THE DEVIL MADE THE SMALL TOWN

by

Dorothy Lyons

Kilkerrin House

To

All Those Dear Shades

Who Likely Are Shaking Admonitory

Fingers At Me

```
B LYONS L
Lyons, Dorothy.
The Devil made the small
  town
```

THE DEVIL MADE THE SMALL TOWN
by
DOROTHY LYONS

KILKERRIN HOUSE

1983

SANTA BARBARA

GENESEE DISTRICT LIBRARY

Copyright © 1983 by Dorothy Lyons
All Rights Reserved

Printed and bound at Kimberly Press, Santa Barbara
Art work and cover montage by Susan Salladé
First Printing August, 1983

Library of Congress Catalog Card Number 83-81479

Lyons, Dorothy M. The Devil Made The Small Town

ISBN 0 - 9611728 - 0 - 0

PREFACE

Once I said to Connie, my closest friend, "People keep saying I ought to write the story of the family, but I don't see how mine is any different from any others." She shot me a startled glance and after a moment said only, "Oh! brother!"

Through the years my kin has urged me to put down some of the family anecdotes, all of which were told me by Mother whose prodigious memory gets most of the credit. Now at last in my seventy-fifth year I have done so lest they be lost with me and the young members be cheated of any feeling of family, or think that it sprang full-blown in the 20th century. In some instances I have dressed up these stories (or legends) — maybe fleshed them out is more accurate.

The community where my family and I grew up could be Everytown or Anytown, U.S.A. Since those Toonerville cartoons of so long ago, the name epitomizes America's small towns and I have used it as such.

I am sure there are errors and misstatements as in all works that depend on that frail instrument, the human memory, but I have kept it as accurate as I could. A few times I may have mixed names up harmlessly, and in some instances I have deliberately changed names to protect the guilty.

Possibly the readers' biggest problem is that the entire work is organized by subject rather than chronology. This means sudden changes of time and place and, perforce, some shifting back and forth, but if you will just "roll with the punches" it will all blend into the whole.

Bon appetit.

The Devil Made The Small Town

I

"God made the country; man made the city; and the devil made the small town," a maxim I learned in Sociology I, was never truer than in the small Michigan town where we and our parents before us were born and lived. "Toonerville," we called it with affectionate derision, and so loyal were its sons and daughters the name spread far beyond its expected bounds due to two world wars and the communications expansion.

There was probably more devilment to the square mile than you'd find in a day's driving — and this refers only to young folks' hell-raisin' without any regard for the more sophisticated and studied senior sins. Happily, that period before and just after WW I was curiously innocent and the horrors of drugs and the attendant tragedies were unknown. But what of the root stock that bred it?

Grampa Lyons — Patrick Vincent O'Lyons really, came over from County Cork, Ireland about 1846, probably toward the end of the famine. We never had any idea whether or not any relatives survived on the Ould Sod, but P.V. apparently never heard from any. He had little love for his mother country aside from the inevitable nostalgia and missing what friends if any were left. Very occasionally he had scraps of news through a neighboring Irish family.

Upon landing in New York's melting pot he soon learned there was a war going on, but it was no private fight, anyone could join, in fact they'd pay you to do so. An opportunity too good to miss. He and a friend went into a recruiting office. The sergeant in charge was always glad to see two young Irishmen: they made good fighters, were generally tough and could stand the rigors of a long, hard campaign. Which it was, with supply lines stretching from New York City to Mexico and almost beyond.

"What's your name?" he asked P.V.

Gramp thought fast. Here he was in America, about to join its army, and b'gorra he was going to be an American!

"Patrick Vincent Lyons."

A few more questions and P.V. was swearing allegiance to the United States of America and things couldn't go fast enough for him to get to Mexico into the fighting.

He almost got more than he could handle, for in storming the heights of Chapultepec a bullet bounced off his skull. A few years later with more sophisticated armaments it would have finished him. It did, of course, make a hole in his head, how serious is not on record, but thereafter he had a silver plate. His sons recall that whenever he was going out to work in the heat he spread grape leaves in his hat to cool the plate lest the conducted heat fry his brain (in the real sense, not the modern connotation). Not long after this, peace was made and the Treaty of Guadalupe Hidalgo signed. So there was Gramp without a war to fight.

His Irish luck didn't desert him, however, as the brass decided to send his regiment to San Francisco where gold had been discovered and keeping the peace was no small task. He just about got his fill of fighting in that brawling, drinking, hardliving — and hard dying — town before his enlistment expired.

Then he and his Irish boat friend Dennis McGuire bought themselves shovels and went out prospecting for themselves, finally staking claims near Banjo Flat on the North Fork of the Cosumnes River. Every panful was a thrill; every shovelful an adventure, and while they never made any big strikes they did consistently well and their pokes got fatter and fatter just on a steady day to day basis.

Law and order were still just words in a big book.

Every morning's sun rose on dead miners and their empty, or vanished, pokes with the authorities as perplexed as anyone as to the murderers' identities. It didn't take long for Gramps and his friend to get the message. "We'd better get out of here with our pokes while we're still alive."

Get they did and in the course of time showed up in the Tyrone area south of Toonerville where the other man had friends. (Oh, no! They couldn't have detoured down through Southern California to woo and win one of its fabled senoritas and make me a landed Native Daughter!)

Gramp apparently had no direct contact with Ireland as he had never learned to read or write. It was not that he was stupid — he just never had a chance to learn — which made keeping the family ties alive chancy. Dad was always ashamed but I relish the thought that my books have been on sale in the country where he did not have the opportunity to learn.

With some of his gold he purchased 120 acres of green, rolling countryside with a creek running through it — probably a good deal like what he had left in Ireland, but here it was *his*. A quick dwelling, principally logs, sheltered his new family but not for long. Gramp was a do-er and soon he had the first frame house in Livingstone County. It still stands out back on the Lyons Centennial Farm and some of its carpenter work which is almost cabinet quality amazes builders to this day.

Gramp and his wife had eight children in what was so common on the frontier, his first family. They all scattered when their mother died. He married again, this time my grandmother Hannah Sweeney, one of the neighborhood lassies, and to them seven children were born. Their first born, Edward died in his early teens of diphtheria and although it advanced my father to eldest status he felt his brother's loss so keenly he was never really able to talk about him.

My mother was from the impecunious Adamses, some

kin of Sam, mother always said, who had arrived in Michigan by way of Connecticut, western New York State, Canada, and thence into Michigan.

Each stopping place represented a generation as the younger ones began to wonder what was beyond the hill and move on. Their first stop after Connecticut was in western New York State, Adams Corners, we were told. Family ties were not broken by this westward movement, however, and later some of the eastern branch traveled to Adams Corners for a visit: mother, father, and grown daughter, Ruth Barbour/?Barber.

Ambrose, the young man of the house, fell deeply, wildly in love with his cousin and did everything he could think of to impress her. It was not easy, however, as she was already betrothed to a sterling young man back in Connecticut, this trip being by way of a holiday for her before settling down to the serious career of marriage.

When time came for the visitors to leave for home Ambrose could not stand it.

"Oh, please do stay on for a visit, Ruth. When you're ready to go home we'll see that you have safe travelling companions — if no one is going one of us will take you. Oh, Uncle, do please let her stay a little longer."

"What will Jonathan say?" her mother queried gravely.

"Oh, he'll be all right five minutes after we meet again. Please, Mother."

Ruth, who had been preening herself a little on the conquest of her cousin, added her urging to his. At last and against their better judgment, her parents consented to the arrangement and left for home. The young girl's excitement at staying on was dampened by the leave-taking and once they were gone Ruth began to visualize the hundreds of miles between Adams Corners and home; long, hard, often dangerous miles, but the excitement of a barn-raising, two weddings in which she visualized herself in the leading role, and a series of midsummer festivities soon cheered her up.

The weeks wore along and gradually the face of Jona

than, her affianced true love, became plainer and dearer to her. By then it was coming on autumn and no time to begin an arduous journey through virgin wilderness. Winters, it turned out, were no better than Connecticut winters, and Ruth found herself longing for spring when she could start home.

Ambrose's ardor had not dimmed one bit, rather it seemed to intensify, and Ruth was driven to evasive action. The earliest hint of spring triggered her first request for travel arrangements.

"I'd like to take you now if I could," Ambrose regretted, "but there'll be all the spring plowing and crops to get in. Once that's done there might be time."

Ruth patiently participated in all the family chores and activities. When the brown fields looked perfect and complete, she renewed her request.

"Why didn't I think of that before," Ambrose exclaimed. "Now I've started digging this new well. We do need it though and it can't take very long."

The homesick girl felt a cold core of fear way inside her, but she bided her time. The next time she asked there was some other pressing project. And the next. And the next. And the next. Each time Ambrose renewed his more and more impassioned suit.

"It can't be all that impossible to find your way along a plain trail," Ruth mused. "I'm going to try it!" She began to secrete bits of equipment she could use and food staples to take. Suitable clothes presented a problem. Having heard about Indians, and ruffians, desperadoes that frequented the trails, Ruth concluded the thing to do was wear boys' clothing, and under the guise of needing them for field work she accumulated an adequate wardrobe.

One dark night under cover of a threatening storm she slipped away from the Adams homestead. The dangers and terrors of that night and the following day were too much for her ever to recount. Ambrose was already in the field cultivating the new young corn when her absence was discovered.

Incoherent with anger and fear for her safety, he unhitched his best mare and galloped off down the trail without even stopping at the house for supplies. Ruth had had one encounter with a noisy group she was able to hoodwink only to run a-foul of some real rascals who immediately saw through her disguise, if disguise it could be called when her thick hair and swelling curves proclaimed the lie of her masculine apparel.

"Ho, ho," the leader crowed. "Come here and tell me about it, missy," he said with mock concern. When she refused to, he grabbed her in his arms and was about to plant his hot, wet kiss on her lips when Ambrose burst upon them.

Hell hath no fury like a spurned suitor, giving him the strength of ten which soon routed the bullies who had only been looking for some fun. Ambrose picked her up and set her on the broad, bare back in front of him, but even her deliverance did not soften her toward this man who had tricked her.

"Don't you even have a smile for your hero?" he chided. "Or thanks for saving you from that scoundrel?"

"Not until you take me to my parents' doorstep." Her aversion was plain despite the catch in her voice.

But he never did and family accounts stated that she was never known to smile, not at least until seven children and eighteen years later she was dying and saw her escape at last.

Her eldest son Simeon married Alfreida Britton at Adams Corners. She was a granddaughter of David Britton of Westmoreland, N.H. who had moved there from Massachusetts where he and his family had been ardent patriots (and any wishing a sure-fire ticket into the DAR or SAR need look no further).

Nine children were born into this family. Jason, the eldest, reportedly lived in the Chelsea section of NYC where he operated a circus. Ambrose, the second born, was afflicted with itchy feet and left the family home before he was very old. He wasn't much of a correspondent, so news of his wanderings was sparse. The latest heard about him was that he lived in Socorro, N.M. but this was third hand. Alfreida, of course, grieved not to know more about her son's whereabouts and welfare.

Very early one summer morning she went down to start the fire for breakfast before anyone else was up (she liked the peace and serenity of this time of day before the younger children were around) and found a tramp sitting on the front stoop. This was not unusual for times were a little hard and many unattached men took to the road. This one looked all right, clean and neat, his beard nicely trimmed and clothes clean though not new.

"Good morning, ma'am. I wonder if I could have a bit of breakfast."

"Well, you'll have to work for it. Isn't ready yet anyway — as you can see," she replied testily.

"Oh, surely, ma'am. What would you like me to do?"

"Out there around the corner of the barn is an ax and plenty of wood that needs splitting up into stove lengths. Bring me an armful when you get it done and I'll feed you."

Alfreida went about the business of getting breakfast. Occasionally she would stop to listen to the ax the stranger was plying with a will. By the time he brought in not one, but two armloads, breakfast was all ready.

"Here, sit here at this place. The young'uns won't be down for a bit." She dusted some imaginary crumbs before setting his meal in front of him, salt pork, eggs, fried potatoes, homemade bread & jam, a cup of coffee, and for good measure a slice of apple pie. "You did good work. You must be hungry."

"That I am — and this is just such a breakfast as my own mother used to give me."

"Where you from?"

"Pontiac yesterday, but I started out from Socorro, N.M."

"You did! I hear my son Ambrose lives there. Did you

ever hear of an Ambrose Adams? About your build, same color eyes, beard a little darker, a mite heavier too — or used to be."

"Ambrose Adams! Of course, I know him well. One of my best friends — most of the time."

"Oh-h, how is he? Is he well? Getting along? Is he married? Oh-h, tell me." Her knuckles whitened with the intensity of her emotion.

The young man looked into her face for an instant. Tears came to his eyes.

"Mother, don't you know me?"

Ambrose stayed home for several weeks before starting the long, long journey back to Socorro and that was the last they ever saw of him. Much later a report filtered in that he was dead, killed by his partner in a mining venture but no one ever knew for sure.

Mother was born in Windsor, Canada, but not much later her father decided distant fields were greener. Entering Michigan at Detroit, grandfather was looking for good farmland. He turned down one parcel offered him, "Miserable soil, too swampy," and bought fifty miles from the rejected plot which is now across from the Detroit City Hall. The farm he bought is still what it was, a good farm.

Mother, Mary Louise Adams, was a local beauty in the same high school class with Dad who found courting a local belle uphill work when he lived twelve miles out in the country — by horse and buggy. The story was told that one night after Dad called on Mother he was on the way home, so tired from his field work he could not stay awake another minute.

Tying the reins around the buggy whip to keep them from dangling on the horse's heels Dad leaned back to relax. The gentle evening air after a hot day, the rhythmic motion of the buggy were soon more than he could fight. The sandman claimed his own.

Dad awoke with a bright sun in his eyes, the horse patiently standing at the gate — but what gate? Somehow he had turned himself around and gone back to where he spent so much time, Mother's gate, where he waited quietly for whatever came — it is alleged.

Despite having been high school sweethearts, Mother and Dad were not able to marry for many years (several anyway which probably seemed like many to Mother) while Dad struggled to achieve a solvent basis for marriage.

Dad proved himself a leader from the start (Mother was always sure that but for bad luck he could have been president — I wonder! To him white was spotless white and black was inky black without *any* gray areas). He was senior class president in Literary School and, as such, appointed a Committee to Investigate the Desirability of a Uniform Garb for Graduates. Caps and gowns were decided on and his led all the rest at Commencement, but did any of us wear this Number One outfit to graduation? No! Some local yokel many years later borrowed it for a fancy dress party and — right! It never got back home.

Dad completed Law School the next year — there were many hiatuses throughout his schooling while he took time out to earn enough to pay his way.

On graduating from Law School he bought a law practice from some charlatan who took his money and never produced a practice.

Dad then turned to bookselling to recoup only to contract typhoid fever while out beating the bushes for the last nickel. A long convalescence postponed things even more, but at last the happy day, or night for they were to be married in the evening, arrived, December 22, 1898.

Mother was the perfect blushing bride, ash blonde now called platinum, peaches and cream complexion, hazel eyes and the figure of a ballet dancer.

After the ceremony they and a few select friends were enjoying — at least the friends were — the wedding feast. Dad was worrying about train schedules on a night of a full-scale blizzard and Mother was having trouble savoring the culmination of years of hoping and planning. She shivered involuntarily.

"Cold, my dearest? Let me get you a wrap. This is probably the worst storm of the year."

"No, Dan, no. I'm all right. It's just — just —"

"What, Louie? Someone walk across your grave?"

"Oh, don't say that, Dan! I have a foreboding, a presentiment something terrible is going to happen."

"Nonsense, you're just keyed up, my sweet. Everything's going to be all right. As soon as we finish eating I'll go to the hotel for my bags, come back here to pick you up and we're off on our honeymoon. I just won't let anything happen to you."

"Please do be careful, love. It's you I worry about. It's a premonition of evil; do be extra careful."

Not long afterward my father called a cab, horse-drawn in those days like a little box on runners and even the driver was closed in with protecting curtains against the storm. The horse jogged along through deserted streets, with Dad immersed in his rosy daydream. Progress was slow because of the poor, almost nil visibility. Dad finally came back to the present.

"If we don't get moving, we'll miss our train."

He put his face to the window to jog the cabby's apparent somnolence but his heart stopped with terror. They had come to the railroad crossing and right above them through the blinding snowflakes was the even more blinding headlight of the Red Ball Express. In that instant on the very verge of the tracks, the cabby realized their danger.

Providence was with Dad — and Mother — for the driver was an old, experienced hand. Grabbing the reins with fists of iron he hauled up and back on the horse that by then knew its danger. The mighty pull lifted the animal off his front legs in a towering rear. Another — or the wind from the rushing express that thundered past just inches away from the horse's thrashing hoofs —swept him back onto the cab to safety. The three of them, Dad, the cabby and the horse, were immobilized with shock as the coal car, baggage car, freights and caboose clattered past, their din dimmed by the cushioning snowflakes.

Horses and harness were no secret to Dad, so between them he and the driver calmed the horse and reassembled the broken bits of harness sufficiently to complete the trip to the hotel.

"Wait here. I'll be right down," he told the cabby.

When Dad returned, however, a few minutes later the entire equippage had disappeared into the storm, too shaken evidently to continue normal activity. Without much trouble another cab was found at the hotel's stand and Dad returned to his bride and the party.

"Dan, whatever's the matter. You look strange — I hope you're not coming down with something — I knew it — I was sure something was going to happen." Mother was almost in tears to be on the brink of her long-delayed honeymoon only to have her bridegroom look so strange.

"It's not 'going to happen.' It already has! And you were nearly wife and widow minutes apart."

He quickly recounted his providential escape from death to the horrified wedding guests. Before Mother could have the vapors Dad got things going.

"Come on, Louie, are you ready? We haven't much time — our train is only a few minutes behind the express, it just has to come from Durand."

He bustled Mother and her belongings together without giving her a chance to ponder the "what-ifs." The well-wishers and rice and ringing good wishes soon chirked Mother's spirits up.

So they lived happily ever after, or at least several years past their golden wedding anniversary.

II

Their children, my older sister, Leona Patricia ("Pat" to everyone but me, then Nōnie with a long ō, the closest

I could come to Leona) and my brothers Donald and Rolland, "Bob," were born to this union of Mary Louise Adams and Daniel Franklin Lyons within four years. Then Dad wanted to call it quits.

"Don't you think three is a big enough family, Louie?"

Not Mother! She'd set her heart on a golden-haired, blue-eyed baby girl and she was not going to be short-changed. She even called her shots so tellingly that a short time after my birth one of the town's leading matrons drew up before the house one afternoon with her carriage and matched pair and coachman.

"How very nice of you to call, Mrs. X. Do come in out of the cold."

Mother graciously drew her into the warmth while the coachman blanketed the horses (I was born in December). Seeing this precaution for a lengthy stay Mother's hopes for a short visit thudded.

They discussed many things, had tea (which Mother was able to whip up on a moment's notice), covered the weather that day, the week before, the forecast for the following week, and when just about every topic had been run into the ground Mrs. X drew a big breath and asked in a rush.

"Oh, Mrs. Lyons, how did you do it? I've had two sons and I want a daughter so bad. Please, please tell me what to do. I'd do anything for a sweet baby girl like yours." (Me!)

Mother's answer is classified information.

My popularity was pretty low in some quarters as was to be expected. Dad's enthusiasm was less than tumultous and Bob, the brother four years older, had no intention of abdicating his place as dear little Rolland. Grandma Adams, Mother's mother, had been there when Bob was a baby and as the result of an accident made a real pet of him.

Farmers' sleighs or bobsleds had two big runners and a favorite sport was catching a ride by standing on one, the back one where if you fell off there wouldn't be a second one to run over you. When hardly more than a baby Bob saw the big kids doing it and tried to copy them, but no one had told him about the *back* runner, so when his baby foot slipped the other big old runner went right across his toes. The big toe took the punishment, was broken and, from constant exercise never healed until finally the bone began to decay, "mortify" they called it. Removing the bone was the only thing to be done, said the doctor, and so it was done — under anesthetic, of course.

Daily dressing changes had to be without benefit of painkiller of any kind (there weren't many seventy-nine years ago). Mother just had to steel herself to the task, but Grandma's tender heart was torn by his screams. She betrayed her Welsh background by saying "Oh, the poor bye. Oh, the poor bye." Whether it helped or not I don't know but Bob recognized the sympathy in her tones so he began screaming, "Oh, the poor bye." Probably didn't help Mother keep her cool.

Mother was always my fortress and my refuge. Next to her stood Aunty Garber, a great-aunt, my maternal grandmother's sister. Their father had been one of the very first railroad engineers; after all, the steam engine began in England. (Here in my house I have the rough pine chest which he kept in the roundhouse for his belongings with a brass plate stating Rich[d] Cox, Engine Driver.) He had railroaded on the continent (another great-aunt is buried at Amiens), and in England before going to Canada where the booming frontier spirit outstripped good sense. Not long after his arrival, leaning from his cab a telegraph pole set too close to the tracks bashed his brains out.

Great-grandmother was left in a strange land with two little girls, no friends and no money. She never got a cent from the railroad; a newspaper article made it look as though he had fallen from the cab and sustained his skull injury in that manner. (Yes, unions do have a place in life!) She did the only thing a poor widow could do then, remarry. Her new husband was very strict with her girls (did he want them?)

Aunty had a sweetheart, Billy Wheeler, but he was considered "wild" and not suitable husband material so was sent packing, but Aunty's eyes always had a soft, faraway look when she mentioned his name. (We all think we are guided by God-given wisdom when meddling in someone else's life.) Grandma had better luck with her pick (Grandpa) so when she married at sixteen Aunty went with her very soon.

Aunty helped bring up her family of seven; then moved on to help her eldest niece with her family, and thence along the line until there were no more dirty dishes to be washed nor didies to be boiled. Only then to the consternation of the entire family they found that while Aunty had been drudging along her spirit had been soaring.

"The government has opened up some land for homesteading in the State of Washington. I'm going west to take up a claim. I'll let you know my address."

"Aunty, dear. Will you be all right? Do you think —?"

"I'll be fine. Don't worry." Aunty put her haircloth trunk aboard a comical little train that eventually got her there.

Already in her sixties, she took up her claim on the Olympic Peninsula, Centralia (I think) and lived on it three years until it was all hers. During this time she met a widower, a Civil War veteran considerably older than she but a good match. What bliss it must have been for Aunty to wash dishes, put up preserves, quilt a new coverlet for her own man in her own home in that new land.

The family never met John Garber as he died a few years after their marriage — at about the same time Mother was noising it about that she was going to have this golden-haired, blue-eyed baby girl. Back onto the train went the haircloth trunk and whatever else Aunty had accumulated as she headed back to Louie who needed her.

She was a real pioneer woman. Once her remark she always liked to wash the dishes in order to get her hands into warm water recreated the barren, spartan life when hot water was a luxury not available with the flip of a handle. Some of her little homely hints she passed on to me, never realizing how different life was becoming, like using your middle finger to rub your eye as it was least likely to have germs on it, or if the toilet paper supply was harsh, to scrub it back and forth in your hands to soften it.

Dear Aunty! How I wish now I am grown that I could treat her as she deserved, and make her know how loved she was by the entire clan. She was completely selfless where I was concerned and wanted only to give me pleasure or to relieve any distress.

She lived with us the better part of her life from then on. When Civil War widows were voted a pension we all thought Aunty had it made. Instead of being either penniless, or dependent on what she considered others' largess (far less than wages), she would have her own money. Consternation and dismay followed the revelation that Aunty would not get a pension because Uncle John had had a common-law wife (as many of the early settlers had when too far from a church or minister) and there was no record of her death.

Never let it be said that a Lyons is stumped, however. Dad had a law school friend in Congress then who obligingly wrote and introduced a bill in the House to the effect that Harriet Cox Garber should receive her Civil War widow's pension of $30. per month. One day when things were dull the legislators shuffled their papers to this bill, voted that it should be so, and presto! Aunty became a woman of independent means by Act of the Congress of the United States of America.

Nor did she keep this great wealth to herself. I ate much ice cream I would not have, saw circuses that had been only a poster, took little trips I'd never have had, and every birthday for twelve years she bought me a souvenir sterling teaspoon.

Child experts discuss how early memory begins. I don't know about most people but I do know I can remember one incident when I was two years old. It's easily cross-checked and not something anyone could have told me: during my mother's youngest sister's wedding to a mining engineer (in our home, — the popularity of church weddings for anything but the grandest unions had not surfaced) the minister asked the standing guests to bow their heads in prayer. Dad was holding me in his arms and from the eminence of his 6' shoulder I looked out upon a cluster of bent necks and heads that looked like withered sunflowers or flamingos.

But Aunty's spirit still had wings; her travels were not over. Later this same sister whose wedding I'd attended at age two went to Mexico with her mining engineer husband and Aunty went along. They couldn't have picked a livelier time. Pancho Villa, hero or brigard depending on your outlook, was in the ascendant. One time he made a sweep through their place, stole my aunt's dear riding horse Buck and anything else he could lay his hands on.

I missed Aunty sorely despite my Grandmother being with us then (the only grand parent I can remember). I see now that she was very ill, dying, but her gay spirit could not be quenched and she entered wholeheartedly into a "pretend" I never tired of.

For Christmas I had received the most beautiful dappled gray rocking horse a girl could ever have (I see why I still favor gray horses). As soon as breakfast dishes were done I'd say, "Come on, Grandma, get on. Time for us to go to Mexico for a visit."

"All right, baby. I'm on right behind you."

Grandma patted the horse behind the saddle. With that I'd begin rocking, and rock and rock and rock and rock until I figured I'd gone far enough to get to Mexico. Dismounting, I'd walk up to an imaginary door and knock, whereupon Grandma played the role of Aunty and my Aunt Jen, exclaiming at our arrival with lots of "do come ins" and "let us fix you something to eat." (I have low blood sugar and am always hungry.)

Bless Grandma for her patience. I never tired of the game, and if Grandma did she never said so. Probably if you have cancer make-believe was the least she had to worry her. My only other memory of her — if it was "her" — was being told I couldn't play on the delightful white bearskin rug under her casket.

Another important happening in this era was when the folks bought Aunt Ada's house on the hill where we moved from The Avenue, and this move dates all my recollections before four or after four. Whether Bob wanted me to or not I tagged along with him whenever possible. One day I went with him to the library to get a book.

Here let me explain lest it be confusing, Mother and Dad called me Dorothy, the boys and their friends (and later families) called me Babe, Nonie, her friends and subsequent family called me Snooks (for Baby You-Know-Who).

"You're big enough to have your own book, Babe. Here, come on and tell me which one you like."

We looked them all over and I'm still impressed — and a little surprised — at Bob's good judgment. He picked out "Johnny Crow's Garden" for me and many, many years later while working in the publishing industry in New York City it was reissued.

Stars fell on Michigan! When I learned what magic, what glory, what transports of delight lived between those book covers, I resolved I was going to grow up and write books.

Knowing about books only made more trouble for the family as no seated person was safe from a tow-headed little girl who'd sidle up with a book in her hand, pleading, "Read to me, please. Just for a little while."

When the family's exasperation had just about reached the explosive phase, word filtered in that the South Ward School near our new home was opening two weeks late due to the installation of a new heating system. Why not send Dorothy and let her learn to read for herself? A quick phone call and arrangements were made. Of course, I was only four years old — no matter, I was quick for my age.

Educators talk about "reading readiness" and other psychological factors in sending a child to school but there was no doubt about my reading readiness. I'd already learned the alphabet so when Mother's hands were busy I'd stand near and say, "Mama, does QZ spell anything?" Or JX. Or — If only someone had taken the time to tell me the importance of vowels. What a thrill if I'd ever made a word!

No happier child ever started school than I. So blank disbelief met the teacher's note three years later that Dorothy was having trouble with her reading. I began carrying my reader home so that dad could help me with it.

The first session I began reading glibly, but when he stopped me on a word, corrected it, and then told me to proceed I could not do it. I had to go back to the top of the page. He handed it to me upside down, and after a quick look at the picture, I began to "read" the book.

Regardless of how he handed it to me, once I got my bearings I could recite the whole page, the whole book. I had it completely memorized! All I needed was a guidepost or two to tell which page and away I went. Dad who was with a textbook firm used me many times as a horrible example of the wrong method. Under his not always patient tutelage I learned the phonic system and to recognize words individually and not as part of the whole.

Wonderful though school was it had one serious drawback. Being away from home so long kept me from nibbling to keep my low blood sugar (which I didn't know I had) at bay until I had a great idea. "The Lord helps those who help themselves." A new power pole had been set in the school yard, leaving a foot or so of bare earth around it. I filched a packet of seeds from home and lovingly planted them in that fresh earth.

No seeds ever had been more cherished: every recess I bent over them lovingly and when some little green plants pushed up I was ecstatic. No more starved recesses. Lest someone discover my garden I kept a piece of paper weighted down on top of them and despite the sheltered environment the plants grew. One day I was so carried away with my plan's success I was not careful enough and the two teachers strolling around the schoolyard grew curious about my activities. Their peals of laughter made my whole inspired plan to "help myself" look ridiculous and I've no idea if those radishes were ever harvested. Not by me certainly.

III

In a way Toonerville was a remarkable little town. A prominent family that had had a manufacturing plant there (before it burned down) made several philanthropic gifts to the town. What the others were I cared not, but a building that had been the company office was turned into a library with an endowment that guaranteed all the books one greedy little girl could read.

Those days it was "one card, one book" but as one reader after another grew up and away I fell heir to their cards which permitted me to take four books home at a time. Even so I went through them so fast I kept the sidewalk hot going and coming with new loads.

One blustery winter day I had finished my last book and needed replacements. When Mother heard I planned a trip downtown to the library (maybe a mile) she tried to dissuade me without success, so failing that she bundled me up like one of Byrd's men. The town seemed strangely silent and vacant but I little noticed as I beat my way through the snow.

How chilled I may have been by the time I arrived

there was lost in a towering rage on discovering the librarian had not come to work through the blizzard. I left my books inside the screen door and went stamping home in a snit at delicate lady librarians.

Dear Miss Williams, how much I owed to her, for ordering books on my "most wanted" list, for listening to all my wild schemes and hopes, for gently correcting my pronunciation of words I knew through reading — such as "sue" and not "sigh-ox" for the name of an Indian tribe. She had been a classmate of Mother's and Dad's but was like many unmarried small-town daughters who earned a precarious living however they could.

Probably she was a little nicer to me because of "the old school tie" though her gentle nature could never have been un-nice to anyone. Pat, my "Our Gang" white bulldog with the black eyepatch, and I were frequently there when Miss Williams took out her modest brown bag supper which she ate at her desk, charging books in and out the while. Pat had only to hear her rustle the paper and he was right there, begging piteously for a crumb to keep him alive. She never disappointed him.

I have often wondered how different my life might have been had I not had that treasure-trove of reading so available. Not that I always read the "worthwhile" books, many were unsuitable but what I did read gave me a broad-based knowledge that frequently confounded my associates.

Another "advantage" we lucky residents of Toonerville enjoyed was one of the very first movie houses. We happily sat through the frequent breaks when the films had to be spliced or rewound. Mother went to prayer meeting each week and Bob and I were elected to drive her down and back with the horse and buggy. While her thoughts were holy, ours were wholly of the hero and whether he could thwart the villain.

Prayer meeting night just happened to be serial night and after a while Mother tired of the financial drain, two kids every week, and said when that serial finished we were not to start another. Several times she asked if it hadn't ended yet, was going remarkably long, etc. but we assured her it was still running.

Finally when she mentioned it to a friend she learned it had ended long since. Turned out it had, but management had run in the first reel of the next serial and we hadn't known the difference. So much for the effect of movie violence on young ones.

Our town was strategically placed with regard to cities. Michigan's biggest city was but fifty miles away on the Grand Truck and Flint another smaller city booming with this new-fangled auto industry was sixteen miles distant. At first fifty by train was easier than sixteen on a dusty, washboard gravel road but later when that road was paved the whole sixteen miles it became more important to Toonerville and its younger residents.

It was fortunate Grandfather Adams had not put his money into property now across from the Detroit City Hall and Dad, who might have invested $1,000.00 in a struggling company headed by Henry Ford, instead put it into a local industry that promptly went bankrupt. Wealth to any degree would have been the ruination of us, my brothers certainly.

When the Devil did his fast talking, they got into enough devilment without money. Much of it was just high jinks such as many small town boys indulged in — tipping over as many outdoor privvies as they could manage on Hallowe'en. I recall watching from our yard one All Saints Day while the town marshall and a squad of boys, my brothers included, retraced their previous evening's route, pushing all the backyard shrines back onto an even keel.

Other escapades were not as innocent. I won't defame my brothers' characters with details but my mother's head of white hair attested to their wayward tendencies. Probably the family lawyer bought many luxuries from Lyons patronage.

It's not that Mother and Dad didn't try to bring us up

right, examples of moral rectitude, industry, application, and a general God-fearing attitude. That's the way they had been reared. What their families lacked in money was compensated for in good thoughts and character building. There was a slight breeze stirring, however, the forerunner of later liberty and license and the permissive spirit that opened up teen-age vistas in so many directions.

Dad travelled the State of Michigan five days a week with only weekends at home. To us stay-at-homes it sounded like a perpetual picnic, staying in hotels (picture the level of service and comfort in pre-WW I country hotels!) the indigestible food, the irritation of having to fit his business appointments to a train schedule (once he wrote the Grand Truck Railway head dispatcher a stiff letter complaining the 9:02 had left at 8:59). Autos later mitigated some of the annoyance and discomfort.

Before leaving Monday morning Dad mapped out what work the boys were to accomplish during his absence, very little of which was done. This meant his first day home was a tense one as the boy's sins of omission and commission came under scrutiny.

Our house on the hill was almost as much a family member as we kids. Situated on a knoll above the street hill it could see and be seen by a goodly area while its two big porches seemed to hold out welcoming arms. A great take-off point for sledding, we would all ride our sleds as far as we could to school, leave them in someone's yard and collect them on the way home. Bicyles went all the way and what a start! There were only five bedrooms plus the finished-off attic so it was "No Vacancy" just about all the time.

The attic was the boys' domain and to reach the stairway they had to go past Mother's door. Very late nights or when they did not want to be discovered their progress from the top of the stairs to the third floor stairs was necessarily very slow. Mother was a phenomenal snorer, embracing just about every variation known, so they soon learned to time their steps along the hall to her thunderous reverberations or the long, sibilant whistle of an engine losing steam. Time consuming but effective.

Except this one time she was determined not to be flimflammed and slept in one of the beds. Bob reached the door first and it took only one step to see the trap. With him was Brownie, his stammering friend. On one push Bob propelled his frient into the room and jerking the door shut, held the doorknob on the outside.

Mother awoke from a sound sleep, her eyes too sleep-filled to recognize details, so she began giving that rascally young fellow, presumably her son Rolland, the very dickens. All Brownie could say in self-defense was a series of unintelligible monosyllables that didn't help his case at all until Mother woke up enough to recognize her hapless target.

There were but three big rooms on the first floor in addition to a small room we used as a dining room/kitchen and a pantry. One Mother said was to be her "Sanctum" and we were to knock before entering. What a joke! It was the busiest room in the house. If we weren't using it for a sitting room as in the winter it was more than anything else hallway to the front of the house; Dad's room which was another big joke as it was where everyone congregated, site for the Christmas tree, dancehall, music room for the Victrola. The one fairly unused room was the parlor though it got a good deal of use when Louise's "fellow" came courting.

There was another floor, half basement set into the hill and half summer kitchen, dining room, laundry and cool room. It was very pleasant to eat down there during a scorching summer but not very cozy and cold as the dickens in the winter so it was almost like going outdoors.

Our vantage point on the hill had one great disadvantage. The house was too vulnerable to winter's cold blasts, especially a strong wind that searched out every entry. The summer kitchen area, open to the north and west, without any insulating earth heaped up around the foundations, was really our Achilles heel.

The big house had central heat but no system had the clout of a howling norther. The pipes always froze, sometimes just a little, sometimes so solid they burst and thawing out time was a mess.

The trouble spot was in the corner of the summer kitchen. Someone long before had spotted it and torn the wainscoting out to expose the frozen earth. That made blowtorching to thaw them easier. Then, as the same problem arose every winter, another dug into the hill a little further and at bedtime would bank the pipes with a shovelful of coals from the furnace.

Occasionally the coals were a little too hot and charred the wood but this was apparently no cause for alarm. They continued to do it and snuggled down into bed with the thought of a warm house and running water in the morning. Until the snappingly cold night Mother sat up in bed.

"Dan, I smell smoke."

"Probably just my pipe smell," he muttered.

"I don't think so. Dan! Wake up. We (good sport, many wives would say "you") "better go down and look."

It wasn't necessary to do more than open the basement door when the smoke and glare alarmed that all was not well. Neither had taken the time to put on slippers or a robe and were barefooted in their shifts. One try showed that the pipes were not operational. The only water was in the outside pump surrounded by a foot of snow.

No time to hang back. Grabbing pails from the laundry they rushed out to the pump, filled buckets as fast as they could and ran back to throw them on the flames. Again and again and again and again they rushed out and back before they could see any slackening of the fire. Even then those devouring flames were reluctant to give up their hold on this lovely old house that would have burned to the ground, frozen pipes and Toonerville's Volunteer Fire Department surely being unequal to the battle.

Not until the last pailful was sloshed into the charred

hole were they aware of their fiery-red feet and legs from the cold and snow. Their bodies had been well warmed but now a new problem arose, thawing and warming their feet in time to avoid actual freezing or chilblains. That made a short night for them, but Mother was up and had breakfast on the table when we came down, totally unconscious of our close call during the night. What a mercy Dad hadn't been off somewhere on a trip! Like everything else, we all seemed to live charmed lives. There were injuries and accidents to be sure but not one anywhere near as dreadful as it could have been.

And then there was the winter when the water lead-in between the house and the street, six feet down in terra firma, froze somewhere along its way. One hundred fifty feet long and, if the pipe froze, the earth too was frozen solid down to it, so what good to try to thaw it?

From about January to early April there was no running water in the house, neither the kitchen nor the bathroom nor the laundry nor the barn. I rode Topsy over to Kit's two or three times a day to water her but how Mother ever managed I'll never know. That outside pump was cistern water, not for drinking, so the makeshifts and make-do must have tried the patience of a saint — my Mother.

Oh, the joy of coming home for lunch that April day and hearing every faucet in the house gushing!

Summertime was loveliness as its best. Mother was an avid gardener and we had flowers everywhere, notably a triple or quadruple row of peonies, and irises, and roses along the driveway from the street to the barn, at least a hundred feet, maybe more. Roses bloomed everywhere together with many, many flowering shrubs, and springtime was deliriously lovely with all the flowering fruit trees adding their fragrances.

The three-floored barn, hay loft (what a playroom with or without hay), carriage (and auto) floor and stalls in the basement with room for pigeons or rabbits or whatever was big that year lent an air of respectability to the lesser structures like henhouses and the "shanty" that served many purposes. Last but not least was the Chic Sale, a three-holer for two adults and a child, lattice well covered with ivy across the front so one could watch the passing scene without being seen. With indoor plumbing the building's most important role was its roof as a landing field from which we could stuff ourselves from the bing (though I don't think they were called that then) cherry tree that grew within ape distance.

Fourteen different kinds of fruit grew on the place augmented by annuals like melons and an extensive garden guaranteed that we would eat well — as long as Mother kept her health, for tilling, planting, tending, harvesting, canning, and preserving were all Mother's province with precious little help from the rest of us — except for maybe occasional big work days when we'd plough or cultivate or spread garden goody. What a work horse she was, and all of it without a murmur of complaint. I blush!

IV

Our first car was one of Toonerville's first. Charley and Nell Scott had a beautiful old Packard built in nearby Detroit but Dad went farther a-field for his first horseless carriage. A friend, Walt Austin (don't make the mistake of confusing these with recent Austins) had an automobile factory in Grand Rapids.

At least it was a factory if you count a modest building with few labor-saving devices. I once asked Dad what year our Austin had been.

"There wasn't any such thing as years in those days, Dorothy. Walt built a car by hand and when that was finished he started another, incorporating what he had learned on the previous ones."

It seems hard to imagine that such a thing of beauty and mechanical perfection could have been made "by hand". I suppose he had a few screwdrivers, wrenches, drills (augers, we called them then) and hammers. Exaggerated by memory, it seems to have been as big as a moving van with a hood as long as a Dachshund.

Basically it was cream with chocolate trim and lo-o-ts of brass. Acetylene headlights gave a good beam of light but as time went on and newer cars had means of dimming their headlights it became awkward. Our black-eyed white bulldog rode on the running board right by the tank but we never were able to cue him in on turning the valve.

A rubber-bulb horn was handy by the driver's hand but if you really wanted to make 'em sit up there was a "mockingbird" pedal connected to the exhaust and with this at full throttle there was no doubt that the Lyons were in the vicinity.

I'm not sure just what year Dad got the car but an indicator is that in 1911 he took it back to the factory (no small feat driving across Michigan and coping with whatever roads were on his flight pattern) to have doors — real doors that opened and shut just like any other — installed.

I wasn't more than two or three but I can still feel the excitement of Dad saying we'd go for a ride after supper. Once he decided to go out after I'd already been put to bed but it was no drawback. I was swept up in an armful of quilts and blankets and bundled into the back seat on Auntie's lap along with the other siblings.

What a tender, innocent era that was when a drive through the fragrant dusk, catching at fireflies, wishing on the first star was such a memorable experience. One stretch of road, the end of the "flatiron" which was a favorite route had been surfaced with cinders from the cement plant making a soft, silent coating. Green, green Michigan woods on either side sent up so many aromas it could have been labelled "Spring." Aunty was always overjoyed if we were heading for that road, "I love it for its woodsy smell," she explained and to this day it is the "woodsy smell road" to me and my friends.

The wonderful, magical old Austin. I've no idea what finally happened to it: when the engine got too old to be reliable Dad let my brothers have it. They, of course, stripped it down — what stony-hearted insensible clod could have demolished that gorgeous body — to make it look like Barney Oldfield's racer. After that I've no idea! I wonder where its bones were thrown — where it rusted into oblivion.

It was a chariot worthy of a king, and if we only had it today it would take a king's ransom to buy it. A nephew who's into old cars sent me a clipping just a few years ago of a dead ringer for our Austin that S.S. Kresge (I believe) had paid $150,000.00 for.

By that time we were into the war years, WW I, that is. Money was scarce but the pattern was set: America had to move on wheels, with engines. All Dad could muster then was one of Henry's marvelous inventions, a Model T. Changing from a behemoth to a tin lizzie was not easy for Dad. He called it the "damn jackrabbit" because of its instant response and its sporting habit of nuzzling into you after cranking, or jerking a foot or two when gears were changed — not shifted, heavens no! Dad variously demolished a friend's gate, the end of our barn, and the hood of the flivver during his adjustment days. Finally they came to terms with each other although it was never more than armed neutrality and Dad wasn't happy until he went back to a gear-shift with Coolidge.

The Austin had been Dad's car as much as a horse that he had fed and curried and cherished, for there were no mechanics in those days who know more than the driver did. He devised his own little scooter for sliding under on his back as well as whatever refinements the period offered.

But the flivver! There was a family car. Trying to keep the boys away from it while Dad was away on his weekly trips was for Mother a labor of Sisyphus that was never ending and one she rarely won against their cunning.

No one had garages yet so the T occupied a section of the barn once given over to buggies and carriages. For those of you who may remember, these big barn doors slid along a series of tracks which meant that though one door was locked an enterprising young man could diddle them around until the one he sought was available. After the folks caught on to this nefariousness they locked all doors.

During part of this time my aunt from Mexico was visiting before and after she had had her baby under American conditions. It is alleged, but I have always disputed it hotly, that once the boys bribed me to go into the nursery, admire the baby boy, and pinch him roundly so that his cries would drown out the sound of the doors being lifted off the tracks and the T driving away.

When Don and Pat — here I must point out that though my sister's name was Leona Patricia and as she grew up she used her middle name. The family always called her Leona and I persisted in calling her Nonie despite threats of physical and mental harm.

Don and Nonie had legal rights to the flivver once when they didn't want little brother tagging along. They almost managed to get away but Bob caught on at the last moment and ran after the car which by then had lost it top. He only succeeded in grabbing the back seat as they started out of the yard, so Nonie did what any enterprising young lady would do: jump in the back seat and hammer his fingers hard enough and long enough until he lost his grip and fell bellering chagrin and pain and frustration into the dust.

Another time Bob outsmarted himself by stealing the car on a Friday while Dad was away. Off toward Linden, the neighboring town to the west, there was a straight stretch of road that paralleled the railroad track and Bob saw to it that he was there in time to race a train. It's not on record whether he won though I doubt it as a crossing at the end ruled out any open throttle stuff.

Dad returned that same afternoon. After dinner — I

mean supper, no one ate dinner at night then — Dad said,

"Bob, I'd like to see you in my room."

"Sure, Dad, what is it," Bob tried to say cheerily, feeling sure that one of his sins had found him out.

"I thought I said you weren't to have the car until your grades are better. I hear on good authority you raced the train earlier today."

Bob was struck almost speechless. How could his father have found out so fast? What stool pigeons were riding with him or observed from a distance? He had to know at whatever price.

"Yes, I did, Dad, but I am most interested in knowing who told you — oh, I'd have told you if you'd asked anyway," he added hastily.

"No one told me. I was riding on that train which gave me ample opportunity to observe the reckless way you handled our only car. If something happens to that, we'll all be on foot for a good long time."

My stock had risen little in the years since my birth. If the family was going, I'd get to go along with little enthusiasm from anyone but that was all right. An automobile ride was a ride was a ride.

Wanting to augment the family fortunes but with no time to "moonlight," Dad had bought a farm to piece out the family income by selling milk and other produce on a profitable market. We never lived on it but it made for many an interesting excursion when he drove out to confer with the hired man or partner.

Possibly the first time Dad realized I was a person with a mind of my own was one day when heading for the farm he detoured through beautiful downtown Toonerville for supplies. I had a tin jackknife, the sorriest excuse for a knife imaginable — probably a prize in Cracker Jack, but it was *mine* (no one else would want it). I whittled happily on my stick during our tour of town and as we turned to head for the farm my hand slipped. The knife flew from my fingers, to the floor and through the door-less door opening to the gravel street.

"Stop! Stop! I've lost my jackknife," I screamed, heartbroken to see my dearest possession disappear in the flivver's dust.

Dad was undoubtedly startled and frightened at my cry. Not so when he learned the reason.

"Forget it. You'd never find it now. No good anyway," he snapped.

I couldn't fling myself out at the terrible speed the T was making. I bided my time and didn't enjoy the farm this time, not the baby calves nor the colts nor the squealy piglets. Returning to town Dad turned from the Avenue to drive up the hill.

"Let me out here, please. I'm not going up home just now," I said resolutely with more calm than I felt.

"Why not? What the hell are you going to do?"

"I'll just walk back to Caroline Street and look for my knife."

Dad stared at me a moment as if seeing me for the first time.

"Oh, all right. I'll drive around that way — but you'll never find it now."

Cruising along slowly, as only a Model T could, I watched the blurring gravel like a hawk looking for prey.

"There it is! There it is. Oh, my knife. I've found my knife." I snatched it to me and climbed triumphantly into the back seat. "Oh, I knew I'd find it. I've got my knife."

The automobile had been the beginning of the machine age. We already had a telephone hanging on the wall with such colorful numbers as 67 Red or 69 Blue, but we were not so keenly aware of the threshold we stood on until a Monday morning Dad saw Mother surrounded by piles and piles and piles of dirty clothes she was going to have to scrub clean on a washboard, those corrugated tin instruments of female torture.

"Fred Granger told me he's just gotten in a machine that washes clothes automatically. I'm going down to get it."

Which he did and later, standing in the truck bed beside this marvelous contraption, he looked like a knight in shining armor to me — and probably Mother. The machine itself was a cause for wide-eyed wonder: a wooden washtub on legs, a little motor set into the top with hoses that connected to the water faucet for power and three fingers underneath that rotated sluggishly one way, then the other. It was a clumsy little apparatus but one of the wonders of the world for Mother who all her life had scrubbed clothes clean by the "armstrong" system.

But the invention that outstripped all else in our hearts was the "talking machine." By this time it had outgrown the horn and had a real name, Victrola. Dad was a real sport, buying a floor model of shiny mahogany, the works on top and a cabinet with shelves for records below. Truly a thing of beauty and endless entertainment.

It was to be everyone's Christmas present that year and there weren't to be any others unless they had been made by loving hands at home. It would arrive and be set up Christmas Eve, but Don had a paper route he had to deliver.

"Oh, please don't open it until I get home."

It was a Christmas card Christmas Eve, a soft, silent fall of snow to cover the ground, to cover the bushes, to cover everything with its impersonal blanket which meant Don must knock at each door and individually hand the paper to his customers. I kept my nose on the glass watching for him until there he was, the snowflakes entangled in his wavy hair and eyebrows, cheeks redder than red and his blue eyes sparkling with anticipation.

Besides this first regulation there were other ground rules: no one could enter or leave the room while a piece was being played (just like a concert hall); there was to be no talking or whispering or rustling during a piece; only the big folks could play the records. I was given a collection of dimestore records which were all I could touch. (I have them yet, little black discs like thin pancakes.)

The Victrola cost $100 which was a tremendous investment for those days, comparable to what, a thousand now? In addition Dad purchased a fine selection of classics, light opera, ballads, comic and Irish, heavy on the Irish which must have run up the ante considerably, considering that just Tetrazzini in her "Swiss Echo Song" was a $5. Red Seal record, on only one side yet!

Christmas morning after our own concert the Victrola was tenderly wheeled into the hall by the telephone. Central soon had us connected with the Cell (short for Celestine) Lyons residence on the old farm in Tyrone while they were treated to John McCormack, then in his prime, singing Mother Machree, Kathleen Mavourneen, A Little Bit of Heaven, I Will Take You Home Again, Kathleen, and When Irish Eyes Are Smiling more than once.

Because of their distance in the country we weren't as close to our Irish clan as Mother's side of the family, part of which lived just down the road, but occasions like this really put strength and feeling into the family ties.

For many years this Victrola lent life and sparkle to our family living, either by producing music for Nonie's and Don's dances, (many's the night I went to sleep to Whispering or Hindustan especially after Warren De-Young, my future brother-in-law came a-courting. For Mother we always had to remember not to play Humoresque or Traumerei when one of her spinster friends was present or she'd provide an obligato of stormy sobbing, why I never really understood.

Another newfangled machine came in a lovely black leather case lined with blue plush stamped with the outlandish name, Blickensderfer: a typewriter. Occasionally Dad let me play with it (words were already my bag) but that brand never caught on. (I'm bound to wonder how it might have fared under a different name.) What made this one so interesting to me was that instead of each letter on a separate type bar there was a cylinder carrying all letters. As a key was pressed the type cylinder raised up, twirled to the proper character and made contact with the paper — the identical way present-day Selectrics do. That would have been easily seventy or eighty years ago; I wonder if some enterprising inventor exhumed those specifications after the patent expired, improved and modified and presto! a new machine.

The machine age was catching us in many ways without our ever suspecting what changes they would bring. Already the airplane was a fact, and after WW I two local flying brothers returned and started their own Flying Circus. Wing walking, flying upside down, loop the loops, falling leafs parachute jumps and other daredevil stunts had their audiences holding their breaths. Bob would have given anything to be able to join but Dad forbade it, and a good thing. One by one these daredevils came to grief until, finally, there was no Circus left.

IV

When I was, maybe three, and Nonie was eleven she had scarlet fever, and the house and premises were quarantined against entry or exit. My school-age brothers were sent to stay with Aunt Ada and her family but being so young I was kept at home — strictly away from the sickroom. Nor did I go out of the yard although I remember sitting right at the sidewalk's edge while a young friend sat on the sidewalk where no germ was supposed to attack him.

As Nonie was getting better and able to be out she used to borrow a burro from my Uncle Charlie who lived a little farther out The Avenue on the original Adams farm. He was our ticket to freedom. With Nonie in the saddle and me behind on the blanket's extension we explored the surrounding territory for all of a mile or two.

Maxwelton (because his brays were bonny) didn't walk fast enough for us to get very far before our deadline but it was a heady experience for a young-one that had never been far from the home hearth.

From the first day forward horses (or equine quadrupeds) became my magic carpet and ruling interest in life. Shortly thereafter when Bob helped me borrow my first book from the library, I knew I'd be a writer and it would be of horse stories.

There were practically none at that time: Black Beauty, of course and a corny little tome called Silverheels were the only real horse stories. Zane Grey and B.M. Bower filled in many arid places with their stories, many of which had gorgeous horses — always stallions. Wildfire — wow! And the black stallion in I Conquered by Bower which detailed the torments of an alcoholic and his attempts to dry up. I drank cup after cup of scalding black coffee with him without complaint if we'd just go out to the horse afterward.

Years later in New York City even my sophisticated roommate agreed that when I dreamed of horses I *meant* horses and not something dark and Freudian. She also said once, "D, you're a pretty reliable girl except when you get with a horse and then I never know when I'll see you."

The family's first horse was May Morning, a spirited yet apparently tractable gray mare, that Dad bought for his bride and their new baby to go driving with. Possibly Mother had some ESP going for her as she didn't hurry to try out the new mare. Of course, it was late autumn and like all thrifty housewives Mother had been canning and preserving as she had for many years.

The first snow had fallen the day before, putting a stop to harvesting the late fruits, so Mother brushed aside any misgivings she may have had and decided to get Leona dressed up in her best bib and tucker and go calling. She hitched May Morning to the cutter/sleigh — its name depending on where you came from.

They went bowling along merrily, the sleighbells jingling and the pretty mare seeming to step in time to their cadence while Mother thoroughly enjoyed her first outing since the baby had come.

"Silly goose," she thought, "why did I ever hestitate to drive May Morning. She's as steady as — as" but her thoughts were cut short by a wild lunge the mare made, followed by a breakneck run, heedless of direction or terrain or obstacles. Mother had handled horses all her life and was not one to panic, but the mare's fright fed on fright until she was uncontrollable.

Later it was learned that a farm they passed had been butchering hogs and the blood smell must have awakened some earlier terror. Mother remembered trying to keep the wildly careening animal in the road but soon it was impossible. She swerved up a bank into an unfenced field. The bump bounced the cutter which might have tracked along but for a big rock that capsized it. Instead of saving herself Mother threw the baby into a snowbank but was caught under the upturned cutter and dragged along like a bundle of rags. Coming to a fence far enough from that terrifying smell, May Morning finally stopped and stood there panting with fright, waiting for a quiet voice to reassure her.

Late afternoon was verging on early evening. Melted snow was turning once again to ice and the westering sun had little effect in the crisping air.

The alertness of a farm woman saved five lives really: Mother from dying under the cutter, my sister in the snowbank during the long winter's night, and three yet unborn.

"Henry, I wonder why that horse and sleigh are standing away over there in that field so long. Seems like anyone liking the view would have their fill by now."

"Where d'ya see it, Em?"

"See, there between those two trees into that next field. You can just make out the sleigh and hardly even see the horse, must be it's gray or white."

Henry squinted as directed until he saw the object of her curiosity, but, his eyes being better than hers, he saw more.

"Good God, Em! That sleigh's upside down. Could be someone's under it. I'll get Jim and hurry on over. Better get something warm going on the stove. If there's anyone there, they'll want something to thaw them out."

Turned out they needed more than just that but it was enough to save their lives and send May Morning down the long road for dangerous horses. Poor mare! It probably wasn't her fault that some stupid man had marked her with this blood terror (but whose, hers or his?) which was all the more dangerous because it lay in her hidden until just the right circumstances triggered it. Then she was a time bomb.

As always happened throughout the family's crises, Dad was on a trip. The baby was all right but Mother had been scraped along on her face on the hardened crust of snow which completely removed all the skin. The neighbor who was drafted to look after them was sitting knitting under a lamp when Dad came running in from the midnight train. He bounded up on the porch, opened the door and closing it stood with his back to it, his face a mask of worry.

"Will she be disfigured for life?" he asked, not will she or the baby live or any one of a dozen other questions he might have asked. Mother was always a little miffed about this.

But she wasn't disfigured, her skin growing in without a mark just as soft and pink and white as it had been before.

Their next horse had been a present to Mother and Dad from his folks in Tyrone, a big, long-striding buggy horse named Doc. Steady as a church he did the family's bidding through all crisis runs for a doctor, on pleasure jaunts, on business trips until he became a real family member. (He must have had some age on him when presented to the budding family because he was always known as Old Doc.)

When I was four he was just seven times my age, twenty-eight, but still an honest deliverer of the goods whenever asked. It was about this time Dad bought the farm two miles out in the country where there was milk for the young family by the cowful, but how to get it?

"Dorothy knows how to drive. Don't you think she could drive out in the country to get the milk?" one said.

"We-e-ell, I suppose if she can turn in the yard Bill could put the milk in the buggy and head them back towards town."

In those days autos were not a menace nor was there the threat of evil, warped people to prey on children. So it was decided that Dorothy should drive Doc out through the summer afternoon to get our milk supply. I was elated to find myself a working member of the family so soon and was very impressed with my own importance, a fact undoubtedly not lost on Bob.

For awhile all went well until Dorothy proved she belonged to the modern generation with its craving for speed. My bubble burst after a neighbor along the route put in a frantic call to 67 Red, the Lyons residence.

"Lou, Dorothy and that trotting horse of yours just went by here like Dan Patch with her laying the whip across his rump. Should I do anything — if I can?"

"Grab them on the way back if you can. Otherwise I'm sure Old Doc will come home — though how fast I don't know."

There ended my career as the little milkmaid.

Despite his years Doc had plenty of pizazz. One winter day Louise, a cousin who lived with us for many years, was going to the station to meet her father's train.

"Louise, don't drive Doc right up to the station. He's terrified of trains. Better tie him on Caroline Street and walk on. It's not far."

"I'll be careful," Louise promised with deceptive meekness, and forthwith drove Doc hitched to the cutter right up to the station platform. Uncle Jim arrived, stowed his grip in the boot and got in beside Louise. Had they been a minute or two faster all might have been well, but at that moment the train was ready to pull out. With a few hoots that sounded like a dragon's war cry, the train blew smoke and steam in every direction and began to roll.

That was too much! Doc was sure it was after him, but it would never catch any kin of Dan Patch, not while he had the use of his legs. Doc got a nice grip on the bit and took off at a dead run. "Forget that trotting stuff, it's every man for himself," Doc decided. The first corner they whirled around on one runner but the next not so good.

Both Uncle Jim and Louise were thrown out and Uncle Jim broke his hip, often the death warrant for an old person in those days, but not an old Cheekako of the Alaskan Gold Rush. Louise was all right but never again a coachman. Doc had slowed down and stopped once he left that horse-eating monster behind.

A good horse like that deserved a better end than his: some low-down, no-good neighbors borrowed him for a trip they had to make and just about drove the old horse to death. Several of us were there at his end picking grapes from the vines that bordered the pasture. Nowadays a good vet might have saved him, it was mainly colic I feel sure, the Number One horse-killer then and now, but nobody knew what it was nor what to do.

He turned around and around, lay down and got up, groaning piteously all the time, until finally the internal pressure on that staunch old heart was too much. It stopped.

After that we had a succession of horses all of which had some glaring weakness of character or body. Queenie was a fine riding horse but in harness she'd make kindling of any vehicle. She had kicked so many buggies to pieces there was no chance of a local sale. All was not lost, however, as WW I was in progress and word went out that the Army was going to buy horses in Mason on such and such a day. Mother and Bob put their heads together and decided he should ride Queenie there and put her into the sale. How I envied him, not knowing my chance would come. Of course, it was more than a day's ride; how they handled this I don't know. Possibly one of our many friends or kinfolk was strategically located.

Queenie was judged sound and a good mount and the Army paid good money for her. Many times I wondered how this little mare, nowhere near big enough for charger material, her only sin that someone butched up teaching her to drive, made out in the rapidly mechanized Army.

Later when I heard a troop transport filled with horses had been torpedoed and the ocean was full of drowning horses my thoughts recreated many of our happy moments. Had hers?

Dollie was a nice little bay mare but she had heaves. Bob tried heaves powder, watering her hay, all the tried and true remedies (if there is one for heaves) but none worked and she too went down the road.

Dynamite was a bag of bones held together by stiff, wiry hair that had literally been saved from the glue factory by my uncle when he heard Bob was looking for a horse.

"He's old, Bob, but he's sound as far as I can make out. There's not a mean hair on him — actually he's a pretty gallant old fellow and you can have him free if you promise to take good care of him."

"Sure, sure, Uncle Charlie. I'll be careful of him," Bob promised feverishly. He was so horse-hungry he'd have sworn black was white.

We had Dyny for quite a while and he picked up some weight and shed out that dreadful coat. But Bob fancied himself as a horse-trader and eventually Dyny went down the long road. Kit and I thought about him a long time and hoped someone good had gotten him.

We were part monkey in those days and climbed any tree that happened to get in our way. A maple tree in front of Kit's house was a particular favorite, so way high, high up in the top I carved the name "Dyny" and the date (I suppose it's there yet! The tree is). We would climb up there and say a prayer for Dyny to get into Snug Harbor. I still hope that two little girls' prayers softened things for him a little.

Years later while working in New York City I answered an ad in the New York Times Personal column to share a beautiful, black, privately-owned saddle horse in Central Park. Of 106 answers the owner chose me to ride Jingo after a trial spin.

Love didn't mean knowledge, however, and later when Jingo went lame his owner asked if I was careful to change his leads.

"Oh, I am particularly careful of that," I replied almost too quickly, then raced to the New York Public Library for a book on horsemanship. Turned out leads weren't something like horse clothing or tack, but a way of going at a canter.

I was getting $18.00 a week (now the deepest depths of the Depression) and he cost me $15. a month but I never begrudged it. I found that drinking an extra glass of water for lunch helped fill me up. Finally when Miss Stiles nor I could stretch a reluctant dollar any farther, Jingo went to friends in the country.

A short time afterward while eating breakfast with my apartment door open I saw a woman in riding clothes in the hall. I asked my landlady about her. "That's Miss Aldrich! Why haven't I thought of her before?" A word to her and soon I was helping exercise Lucky, her bay gelding, free in Prospect Park, Brooklyn.

Shortly thereafter my longing for a place where the sun was warm, the breezes balmy resurfaced and Hawaii became Mecca. Finally I too became one of the blest who made it into Paradise-of-the-Pacific — Hawaii.

There I did buy my dream horse — young, sweet, beautiful with a golden chestnut coat and flaxen mane and tail. I named him Liquid Sunshine, or Sunny, for Hawaii's golden rain that sometimes evaporates before touching the ground. We hadn't been friends very long, however, before he went lame with a succession of bowed tendons so I prevailed upon his plantation breeders to buy him back.

VI

We kids were opportunists but we came by it honestly, for Mother in her own quiet way was always alive to a good thing. When my age was still in one digit Mother heard on her clothesline telegraph about a two- three-acre island in Pine Lake about three miles west of town. Somehow during Michigan's homesteading period this parcel had never been picked up.

Of course, it wasn't good for much but scenery and in the old days the settlers were long on scenery and short on food, so it was never disturbed. Then in 1916 a local drifter learned this fact and was going to take it up, his only progress being a half-hearted excavation for a sod house (no sod of course). How Mother got him to relinquish what rights he may have had to the property is not known.

By then Dad was intrigued with the idea and he began dealing with the government with a view to "taking it up." A wildcat operation had timbered it decades earlier and all but a very few trees were second growth, sprouting up around the old stumps, making its value as a timber claim nil.

Dad did not wish to become involved in a three-year residence, so the government man finally said to make an offer to buy it. Whether offers and counter-offers went back and forth I never knew but it ended with our buying The Island (all it was ever called) for five hundred dollars.

What excitement! What a lark! No one but the Indians and the United States had ever owned it. It was truly an island, making some sort of boat necessary. Dad voted for a motorboat and his was the deciding ballot. This boat,

The Shamrock, is not to be confused with present-day speed boats. It chugged along on what may have been a one-cylinder engine (if that is possible) but we had many stirring rides.

Too it spawned another sport. Aquaplaning on a board behind some sort of motorboat began to be mentioned in the newsreels. So why didn't we try it? Dad and the boys made a board out of a 1x12 sawn in two, fastened together, cleated, a rope attached and there you are. I often rode in the boat but no one wanted the responsibility of a skinny little kid who might or might not be able to swim well enough to look after herself.

Then Don worked out probably the biggest thrill I had ever dreamed of to that moment: the boat was very slow but powerful, other lake traffic was almost non-existent, so one day Don and I went out by ourselves for my one and only ride on the surfboard which is what we called it then.

Inflating my waterwings, he tied them around me, then with the engine on slow throttle he jumped in the water and drifted back to the board. Next I and my wings lept off and Don scooped me onto the board with him. The delirious joy of it! Just like the big kids I was. A passing observer might have had a turn at seeing an empty boat towing two on a board but it was easy to steer by throwing our weight to one side or the other. We cruised and circled and did everything we could devise to heighten the fun of motion, sun, water, summer.

When it was time to stop, Don went hand over hand up the towrope and into the boat. As for me I don't remember whether he steered for shallow water where I could swim ashore or whether he hauled the board up until it touched the stern and I stepped into the boat. I'll never forget the adventure though, partly because it was one and partly because Don cared enough to make it possible.

Just going around and around became too tame for Dad but when a northwest wind blew, making the rollers go streaming across Pine Lake from one end to the other he often headed for the lake and the launch. Bucking the waves was deliciously exciting and sometimes very dampening if the wind-driven spray flew back to soak us but who was to care?

Often we stopped at the farm afterwards, chilled and ravenous. Sometimes the farmer would be milking and those big beautiful shiny pails topped with foaming milk were irresistible. Many people say they can't drink warm milk right out of the cow but they weren't there then, wet and cold. One time I drank twelve cupsful and the last tasted as good as the first.

The Island was out toward Tyrone and it provided the setting for several big, very big, family reunions of the Irish kinfolk. What times they were!

Everyone brought one or two or three dishes to share with the whole family, some of whom we had not seen in a long time. The eating and drinking and funmaking seem now like out of a book. Every mother was an excellent cook, making the air fragrant with baked ham, scalloped potatoes, fried chicken, baked beans (the old way) and the pies — lemon meringue, apple, cherry, blackberry, like as not topped with homemade ice cream out of the freezer that had been grinding along in the background.

Great as the feast was, however, the best part came later when everyone gathered under the whispering trees for a concert. Uncle John's was a beautiful Irish tenor but he was nevertheless outdone by his and Dad's brother-in-law, Rudy. Many of us would stop singing to listen to their "Irish Eyes," "Kathleen Mavourneen," and "Little Bit Of Heaven."

Mother was something of a Wagnerian soprano. Dad had a nice voice he rarely raised in song — possibly by the time I arrived there wasn't all that much to sing about — but my Uncle John's "I'll Take You Home Again, Kathleen" left not a dry eye in the house.

Mrs. K. used to say, "Dorothy couldn't carry a tune in a bushel basket." But I was always singing which was harrowing for the innocent bystanders. Once Mother decided I should have singing lessons.

"Maybe if she knew a little more about it she would do better." Did she really think so or could she just not face the fact that her baby girl had the voice of a crow?

The lessons didn't help, of course, possibly because they were of a short duration. The teacher did not agree with Mother's rationale so I was pitched out into all the sharps and flats with nothing to guide me.

Time went on and I was beginning to accept my handicap until a school production was going to be a musical. Acting I could do but sing! I yearned and burned to be one of the chosen, even to retiring to the hay loft for a little secret practice the day before tryouts which left me little hope.

That night I went to bed early (I had read that singers must have their rest) and as usual sleep met me at least half way. (It's a wonder I never hurt myself seriously by going to sleep the instant before I hit the bed instead of the split second afterward.) Instead of my deep, almost lifeless, sleep I drifted off into a gray haze that soon parted and I found myself somewhere in a lovely forest glade. Flowers dotted the grass, birds sang in the trees and it was all so idyllic I burst into a happy song. Miraculously it sounded good, so I sang on and on.

There was a rustling and murmuring at one side and a majestic figure came into view through the trees. The lady, for it was one, was hardly dressed in conventional clothes. Instead she was wearing some sort of armor, but her face was familiar. It was Mme. Schumann-Heinke in a Wagnerian costume!

"Forgive me for eavesdropping, my dear," who could miss that throaty voice, "but I was so enchanted listening to you I couldn't speak."

"Oh, that's all right, Mrs. ma'm, Mme. Schumann-Heinke," I stammered, almost struck dumb by the glory of it all. "I j-j-just felt like s-s-inging."

"My dear, what a lovely voice you have! Have you had

any training? You really should have, you know, to realize the great potential of your vocal powers."

A miracle right before me. The blinding glory of a life of song. Before I could answer her query about my "training" the bubble burst and I was back in my little slant-ceiling room and the same off-key voice I had always had.

All the years of steak roasts and campfires and moonlight rides filled with song, other peoples songs, and the torture of it. They never knew the words and dum-de-dumed all over the place while I could recite chapter and verse of any song you could mention. The anguish of it!

Maybe if I had taken more singing lessons like Mother wanted me to --------------------?

I have always wondered why these great reunions at the Island did not continue elsewhere. Oh, there were one or two others but not as a regular thing and I always had sort of a cheated feeling that they didn't go on happening. It may have been that Dad lost interest in The Island — and after all it was his family.

Gradually the older kids grew away from The Island but Mother and my friends and I kept on loving it and returning as often as we could. Until Connie and I were old enough to be allowed out there unchaperoned there was always the problem of finding someone to come along. The summer before Nonie married she came out and really joined in the spirit. We had our own song, "This lake of P-I-N-E, Pine, It is so F-I-N-E, fine, etc.", we went hiking on the mainland, we had "swimming lessons" whether we needed them ore not. By this time without Dad's interest and support we were down to a rowboat and one day the last one to step out had not pulled it up far enough. Happening to stroll past the dock I was horrified, electrified to see the boat bobbing gently but tantalizingly well beyond wading depth. I raced up to the Shack where Nonie was writing a letter to her beloved.

"Nonie, Nonie, the boat's drifting away. Come quick!"

"Well, go after it then," she said calmly, estimating my prowess as a swimmer far above what I did. Her word was law though, so I peeled off my clothes and splashed out after it.

A little breeze had come up and I can still see the prow of that boat turning lazily around, rocking so gently only the smallest ripples grew at the waterline but still floating tantalizingly farther and farther. I redoubled my efforts and at last caught up with it, hand over handed along the gunwale to the back where it was easiest to climb in. What a triumphant, returning hero I felt rowing back to the dock where Connie and Kit awaited me.

This was a good warm-up for the Big Event of our camping season — Swimming to the Mainland. The Island was much closer to one shore than the other but the best anchorage was halfway between, making the distance from shore to shore maybe a quarter of a mile. We had been training for this (I honestly don't remember whether the other two tried it or not) and enough preparations had been made for a Gertrude Ederle (who was much in the news about then). The others elected to accompany me in the rowboat. I had been taught to float to rest, the easiest stroke had been decided on.

And The Day arrived. I ate a light breakfast, etc. etc. — and made it easily. From then on I felt more confident when staying on The Island; if I had to I could get ashore.

On and on the golden years went with The Island always there if we wanted our own private Walden. Even after moving away from Toonerville there was always a welcome out there if we needed restoring or recharging. I finished my senior year in college at a very low ebb, so low the doctor said I had TB and should go to a sanatorium. I'll never be sure whether I did or not but I said flatly, "I won't go and if you send me, I'll run away. I will go to The Island though if it can be worked out."

So it was. Connie was to be my nurse/fall guy. We took her red canoe for water transportation with Topsy and a two-wheeled cart standing by at the farmer's on the mainland for trips to town. What a summer! We wrote the bill of particulars for "halcyon." It didn't take me long to begin to feel better; I honestly think I was just exhausted and didn't have TB (altho my lungs show I have had it at some time). My first night there I faded out at eight o'clock not awaking until 1:30 the next afternoon to hear Connie say to a visitor, "She's breathing." Who knows how much longer I might have slept on undistribured?

From then on it was just a long, lazy summer. There was always a breeze even on the hottest days (of course, the breeze was hot) laden with sents of newmown hay or flowers or green growing things, but we hardly exerted ourselves enough to make it uncomfortable. Except one time was so hot we'd soak our suits, put them on and when dry, soak them again.

There happened to be a Boy Scout Camp on the mainland which had some roving councillors in a canoe; we had a canoe and a portable Victrola, Rx for a perfect summer.

What dreams we dreamed. What plans we planned. The one I remember the best was the proper cottage we would build on the site up at the higher end of the Island when we came back as famous authors, and we would call it "Four-Winds Lodge."

We stayed until late September and the frost. One day when Dad stopped in to visit and check on his blonde baby chick (that had started life as The Ugly Duckling) he remarked that the stock market had gone down the drain. And so we eventually broke camp and went back to "civilization" to make our fortunes in the teeth of the Great Depression.

I don't remember whether I spared a backward glance for The Island before driving away. I hope I did, for it was my last time there and nothing can ever match those happy, carefree days.

Many years later it was partly responsible for throwing

me into the arms of the FBI. But that's another story.

VII

As in all small towns our neighbors were a crosssection of the American public. Several were fairly old — according to my standards anyway — some houses were infected with foot itch and no one stayed there long, but some seemed like old settlers. One of these was the Dan Kellehers, as Irish as the Dan Lyons, who moved there a year or two after we moved up on the hill.

Catherine was two years younger than I which provided me with a perfect patsy — a private whether willing or not to exercise my generalship on. A square little face almost always framed by a dutch bob could project the ultimate in stubbornness without a word being said.

I hope I was not too much the tyrant but if I was she has forgiven me. The one nickname that set all her battle flags flying was "Cat-tail" but the other day on long distance she said, "Oh, I'd be so glad to hear you call me Cat-tail again. Do come back to Michigan for a trip."

Kitty, another nickname, wasn't the bravest little person always but if the chips were down she usually delivered. One time we were in sort of a tight spot out on Pine Lake trying to ferry our things across to The Island when a sudden squall hit us with wind and rain. She was in the bow of our sharp-nosed boat and, when the storm hit her in the face, she came running back to huddle beside me. Without her weight up front the wind caught and spun us around.

"You get back up there," I shouted with a Captain Bligh roar. "The wind's already turned us around once."

She started but halfway up it was again too much and she skittered back to me.

"You get up there or I'll — I'll throw you overboard!" I raged, wondering privately just how soon we both might be dunked.

She was afraid of thunder and lightning of which the mid-west has more than enough. Another time we were driving Topsy toward Pine Lake for a swim, me sitting on one girl's lap, Kit on another. Bowling along gaily with no notion a storm was going to hit, a dandy did . . . . come to think of it, it was the same one mentioned elsewhere. The rain and hail blinded Topsy so she ran off the road, down through a small ditch and caught a hub in the fence, breaking the wheel, and ripping the harness apart in half a dozen places.

I jumped for the mare's head as the others ran and cowered behind the buggy for shelter from the driving wind and rain.

"Cat-tail," I yelled, needing emphasis, "Get up here and hold her while I get her unhitched."

Willing as always she started forward, halfway the awfulness of it overcame her, and she scuttled back of the buggy again.

"Cat-tail, you get up here. Right now. Undo that holdback," I shouted and the charm of a particular duty won over.

Wet and bedraggled as an orphan chick she worked her way along the shafts and began undoing snaps and buckles. The other two were a total loss (the last time I included them in a junket!) but between us we got Topsy free from the wrecked harness that could have hurt her had she struggled.

But if I had the Indiand sign on Kit, someone else had it on me. Bob always had me under his thumb — come to think of it both brothers did, but Bob was a plain old tyrant, Don a benevolent despot.

Early one June just after school was out Bob said to me from pure cussedness, "Here comes Cat-tail. Go out there and tell her you don't want to see her any more — not to come again."

And you know I did it! He must have had me hypnotized or else the thought of the swift and sure reprisals intimidated me. No one has to tell an Irishman more than once, so all summer long I played alone. I'd peer through the curtains as Kit walked by or wait until she had passed before going out in front.

"Doesn't seem like you're seeing much of Catherine lately," Mother said. "Did you have a fight?"

I mumbled something in reply which she took to be affirmative. She was not one to mix into children's relationships without an invitation, however, and let me mope around in my solitary state. I surely got a lot of reading done that summer.

September and school was opening. I watched out the side window until I saw Kit coming; I sauntered out the front door and fell into step with her. She looked a question at me. Hanging my head in shame at such craven behavior I explained.

"Bob made me do it."

Her mother, Jen, was definitely a character on a par with all the others Toonerville was peopled with. Lame, she walked with one crutch as a result, I think, of post partum problems. She made it serve her in several small ways. She was maybe the world's worst housekeeper, if not second to me, although she was a good cook. She and Kit helped me prove one of my theories: that children swing to the other extreme from their parents. Kit is an immaculate housekeeper just as children of stingy people are extra generous and vice versa.

Mrs. K as everyone called her, had a sharp mind and delighted in posing world problems whether valid or not to Dad when he may have driven Mother over there.

"Now, D.F.," she'd say in a challenging tone. "Just what do you think of your precious Democrats and their Anointed (Woodrow Wilson)? Don't you think he's making more trouble than he's solving?" or some equally provocative question.

She had a flair for vivid phrases. Once when I gave her some candy, the pale yellow ones made to look like peanuts. She took a bite, chewed thoughtfully for a

moment & said,
"M-m-m, sweetened wind."

She was a compulsive reader but of only one type of book — detective stories. As sure as Kit and I had some important plans Kit would have to post down to the library for books. Somehow Jen had four cards too and new book purchases never could keep up with such an insatiable devourer of the printed word. As a result she had read every whodunit in the stacks over and over and over again. Some she probably had memorized much as I had my reader but it didn't bother her. A few romances she liked if the heroine wasn't too vapid.

No matter what our plans, problems or past happenings, Jen was always interested and listened sympathetically to our tales. In a way Mother was a little jealous of my rapport with Mrs. K. She said to me once, "Why didn't you tell me you had spelled down the eighth grade instead of my having to find out from Mrs. K?" Or, "Mrs. K says your Scout troop is going over Denton Hill on a hike."

It wasn't that Mother wasn't interested or understanding; maybe she always seemed too busy for small talk while Jen was instantly available.

Dan Kelleher was a big, pleasant, slow-moving man. He made a living as a teamster, probably one of the last, and his white team of Bessie and Dewey hauled much of Toonerville's freight. When we were little if he had been hauling (and shoveling) coal. he'd come at us with his black face to scare us. But no one could be scared of Dan Kelleher.

Another neighbor we were always aware of was in the same block with Kit. That was the Baptist Home for Retired Ministers, not that we had anything to do with them but Miss Lou, the matron, was a neighborhood personage.

One year Kit and I were money hungry so decided to pick strawberries for the Baptist Home. Miss Lou agreed to pay us 3¢ a quart and we set to it. Strawberries are better than raspberries, but it took a long time for each 3¢ to pile up. For lunch we went over to Kit's. Afterward we were supposed to lie down in the front room and rest (why then I never knew), when we were on the go every other day. Of course, we were skylarking around instead of resting.

In his big, bluff way Dan came in with the razor strap to pretend he'd give us a licking, but he never got very far. Pat, my white bodyguard, had been lying beside me. One look at Dan's threatening manner and Pat thought it had gone too far. He was a white projectile straight from the floor toward Dan's throat. He threw up an arm and jumped back in time so Pat just lit harmlessly on the floor, although he did nick his arm.

I was scared and upset. Biting dogs got short shrift in those days; I doubt that they were entitled to one bite as them seem to be now. Dan and Jen were jubilant however.

"We'll never worry again about you girls so long as you have Pat with you."

Pat was immediately called into the kitchen where he was rewarded with a treat for his lack of humor.

Miss Lou was a maiden lady of delicate sensibilities. She was once quoted as having said, "Well, when that Lyons girl breaks her neck riding that horse I hope she isn't in front of *my* place." That good old Christian spirit! But she could have been misquoted.

Another neighbor luckily in a class by himself was Sam Dean who lived on the corner of Kit's street and mine. More of him later.

VIII

Mother never learned to drive a car and Bob had only limited use of the flivver, making a horse and buggy required equipment when the pinch was on. After Dynamite and the equally sorry parade of horseflesh that followed him while Bob fancied himself a horsetrader, we were grounded.

Somewhere Mother came by a little extra money, and first things came first. She had to have wheels.

"Rolland, I see in the paper there's to be an auction out at the Lem Farquhar farm tomorrow. How would you like to go out and look at the horses? Lem always drove a pretty good team. If they aren't going too high bid on as nice a one as you think you can get for this much. Maybe we'll be lucky."

"Criminy, Mo--"

"Don't use that word, Rolland. You know it's just a slang word for Christ."

"Well, lordy -- "

"And that's worse. Can't you just speak English?"

"Goodness gracious, Mother! Do you think we could really get a horse?"

"Yes, but be careful. Get some man you know to look it over and make sure it's sound. And ask around to see if it has any bad habits."

"Sure, Mom. Don't worry. I'll get us a dandy."

Mother's face did not show all his confidence, but she could only hope.

How we agonized next day, wondering how he was faring, what the prices were. Some days auctions went very high, others so low it was almost like stealing.

"Mama, do you really think --"

"Dorothy, that's the fifteenth time you've said that. I don't know, and we won't until he comes home. Try to be patient until then. Meanwhile, why not dust the front room?"

That effectively got me out of her hair for a long time as I faded away into nothingness. But before we had any idea Bob could get out there, look around, bid on a horse, and get home, he drove into the yard, leading a spirited, bay mare, slim and trim.

We poured out of the house goggle-eyed at his prize. Walking around the curveting animal at a careful distance we admired every feature, every point from her nervously flicking pointy ears to the trim black legs surmounted by a glistening hide the color of well polished old furniture.

"Gracious, Rolland! How much did you have to pay for this mare?"

"Not a cent, Mother! She's free."

"Don't get smart, young man. I want to know how much — and if there was any change you can hand it over."

Bob read the storm warnings, so he made his story short.

"On the way out to Lem's I stopped at Uncle Cell's and when I told them where I was going, Uncle John said we might as well have Topsy, all she was doing was eating her head off in pasture during the summer and on good cow hay all winter."

As a result of Bob's procuring the mare she was understood to be under his control with my getting only his leavings. This led, it may well be believed, to some stormy times but as time passed and girls developed more allure than a girl-horse, I began taking over.

Topsy, as neat a little bay mare as ever looked through a bridle, had been bought as a foal by my bachelor Uncle John and raised as his pet and a buggy horse. Tyrone's distance from Toonerville meant a good horse made a big difference. However, by the time she had grown up and was ready to take her place in the hotrod ranks the auto had come in which made the trip a breeze.

When I questioned Uncle John once about her antecedents he'd said, "She's pure Hambletonian, girl, traces back to him six times."

Saddles were not too familiar to a harness horse, more a matter of sufferance than familiarity, nor had she ever been taught the rudiments of proper saddlehorse behavior. The instant I raised a foot to the stirrup she was off like a sprung arrow with me, a determined cockleburr, stuck to her side. Many a mile I rode lying flat on my stomach over the saddle on a madly galloping horse until she had spent her energies enough for me to reassert my authority.

So how could I admit to my father (or my mother when she wanted me to deliver a note to a friend if it meant dismounting) that my mastery of this spirited mare was more a matter of chance than skill. Some years later an ex-cowhand, seeing my very real problem said, "Here, sis, just shorten this inside rein a little. Then when she tries to start off with a rush it'll pull her in a circle." Which it did with such momentum it nearly threw me right on over. Hosanna!

Our home place and its three acres with over a dozen kinds of fruit including a sizable vineyard as well as a field below the house grew various crops under Dad's direction. He was ahead of his time in many ways: one I have thought about often when hearing about the hybrid corn that increased the yield so dramatically. Dad was on the trail of that and for several years grew a test crop in our field. Rows were numbered on a chart which recorded growth, ear production, silking, kernel development.

We kids generally walked pretty softly when Dad got up Saturday morning in case he had a migraine, but wherever I might be word would filter down.

"We'll need Dorothy and Topsy to cultivate the corn this morning. Be ready by nine o'clock."

How to explain to my impatient parent that due to the mare's years of idleness she had reverted to an almost-unbroken state, that she had but two gaits — walk and headlong gallop, especially the latter?

My first mount was always chancy and someone else had to have a good hold of the bridle to curb that first frenzied rush. Then once I had asserted my mastery we'd start off along a row, jittering and titupping as though going to the post.

Don, as the brawniest, was always drafted to hold the cultivator handles and guide the teeth between the tender rows of corn. Quite the worst aspect of my role was sitting atop the harness backpad to control the mare.

Ever tried wearing a cotton dress pulled up above your knees and a pair of cotton underpants while sitting on a few pieces of metal surmounting three layers of hard leather? On a jouncing horse!

Under the best circumstances it was an ordeal for man and beast, under the worst a cross between the Inquisition and Indian torture. With our miscues, stops for harness adjustment — or repair, and much-needed rests it took the better part of a day, all of it under Dad's eagle eye.

The horror of the time that the mare got away with me and shot kittycorner across the field, Don at first taking seven-league steps in an effort to hold the cultivator upright and Dad's roars of anger and frustration as it tipped over and raked a swath from one corner of the field to another comes to me yet.

Topsy was honest and game, loyal — maybe, but her affection she reserved for Uncle John. Ours was a business partnership. I can remember not one loving reaction. I doubt that there was any reason for her to love a brat who had no notion of how a horse should be cared for and treated. It's a wonder she wasn't foundered or colicked fatally under our ignorant care.

As an editorial comment I'd like to explain that this was the end of the horse and buggy era, the car had taken over by then, and no one wanted it to be known that he knew one things about a horse. Dad knew, and why he never took the trouble to share some of his horsemanship with me I can only guess: he had so many other problems it just never occurred to him. About the only person in Toonerville whose fund of information came in handy was the local horsetrader, a gentleman whose fondness for the bottle made him dubious friendship material. However, I used to ride with his son and sometimes glean some scraps of information second hand.

16

17

18

19

Christmas 1909

20

21

22

23

24

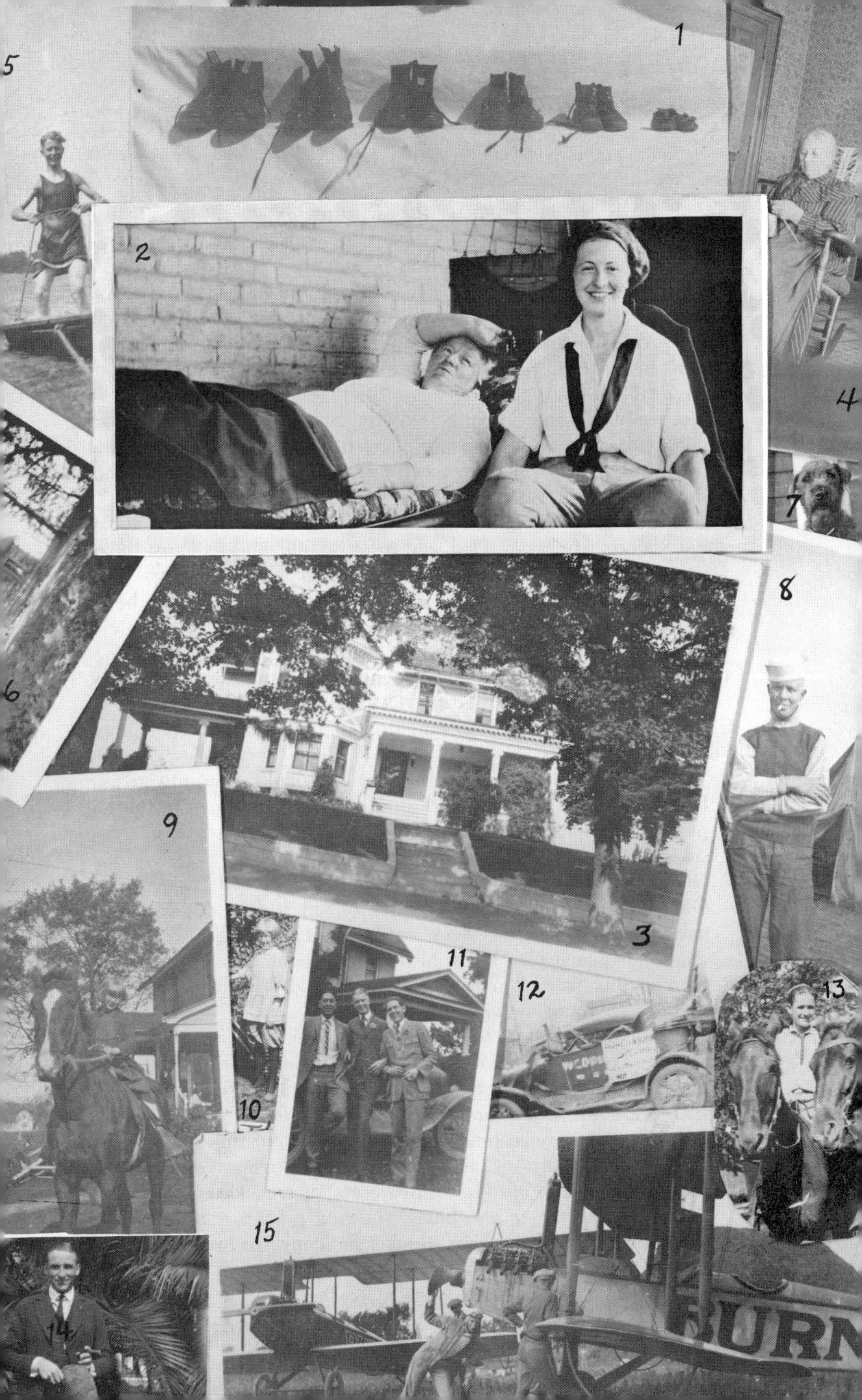
1
5
2
4
7
8
6
9
3
11
12
13
10
15
14
BURN

Key to the Meant

1. Now we are six — just barely, as this family record was taken the month I was born. For this and many of the following snapshots it was fortunate that Dad was an ardent shutterbug which in those days meant you developed and printed your own. He also went in for trick shots, taking one of Nonie's head sitting in a box on a table.
2. Mother and Nonie "taking five" on our sunny, airy side porch during the latter's big berry-picking push to earn money for her trousseau. The porch was everyone's living room during the hot summer.
3. The House on the Hill which is now an Historical Landmark of the State of Michigan. Dad sold it for $3,000. and its latest buyer paid out $150,000. for a place to put his swimming pool. Regardless of its value it will always be valued by us as the home of our youth. From the roof at the right to the bay window was the site of Nonie's death-defying leap.
4. My Irish Grandma, Hannah Sweeney Lyons, who I never knew, in her parlor on what became Centennial Farm much later.
5. Don on our surfboard looking to me like a knight in shining armor.
6. The Shack on the Island, its big casement looking out toward the lake. This and a door were the only outside openings in the log part but the clapboard bedroom section had a window on three sides.
7. Out of her time slot - Kelly Macushla, my beloved Irish Terrier. Once when Don tried to sic her on an itinerant cow, to his amazement she didn't savvy until I explained I'd never had a chance to teach her. I was always calling her off.
8. Don in the Navy. Amazing that he looked so grown up to me then — so young now.
9. Dear old Dyny ready to give his all.
10. Me at a younger age with my very first bike which doesn't show much. Aunty had given me a $5. gold piece which I gladly traded for this little blue bike. It's the only one I ever remember having — must have graduated to horses from there.
11. The Three Dastardly Conspirators who got themselves thrown in the pokey with soon-to-be bridegroom, Warren DeYoung. Taken on the south side of the house showing portico and a sliver of the bathroom window from which Don leaped to the portico roof on a dark night.

12. The Honeymoon Special decorated with its witty sayings.
13. Dex early in our acquaintance while still riding Topsy. Obviously neither she nor Queen Bess think much of proceedings.
14. The Bridegroom, Warren DeYoung, on his honeymoon in Biloxi, far from would be jokesters.
15. Burns Flying Circus in its heyday that accelerated every heartbeat in Toonerville — but especially the feminine ones.
16. Family picture with Aunty too. Bob doesn't show as he is sitting on the ground as you will see in a more complete version on the title page. This was long before the day of automatic picture takers. Dad has rigged a thread around a series of posts and is looking to make sure everyone is ready. (We never know which moments may be frozen in time — or he might have had a collar on though it was a hot day which is probably why they made them detachable.)
17. Topsy, Connie and I in our two-wheeled chariot that was our transportation the summer we spent on The Island. Not stylish but even so short a time after the auto came in, it was already a curiosity to many.
18. Aunty and John Garber, probably their wedding picture and the only one any of the Michigan clan ever saw of him. This one probably required a long trip to town for the occasion.
19. Anyone doubt what I said about Dad not wanting me?
20. Aerial view of The Island several years after we got it when dry years and industrial demands had lowered Pine Lake's level drastically. Originally water lapped at the foot of the trees and I rowed a fairly big boat between the two islands. Here it's dry as dust.
21. Our beautiful Austin on a crisp day with all the ladies wearing hats and coats. Aunty used to fuss and fume about this picture. "Look at that man — his arm around the dog while his darling little girl stands all by herself!" She felt worse about it than I did.
22. Toonerville's main drag a little earlier than the book as it looks as though the street is not paved. Nor would the traffic have been exclusively horse-drawn.
23. Maxwellton of the bonny brays, my first of a long, long line of mounts. If all this picture were visible, however, I think Pat would be up.
24. Old Pat when he was Young Pat being patient with silly little girls, me and a visiting cousin. Dad used to describe my hair (which looks pretty good here) as "straight as a pound of candles and with all the ripe, rich color of a bucket of lard."

IX

"I hear a Detroit millionaire has bought the old Ira Jayne place," Kit's mother, the neighborhood crier, announced. "Going to fix the whole place up. Going to keep horses and who knows what!"

"Wow!" I thought, immediately wondering where my horsey background might fit in.

Time went on. He did fix up the place. He did bring in a gorgeous golden chestnut riding horse with a flaxen mane and tail, "a Kentucky saddler" according to reports. But where I fit in didn't seem to be anywhere.

Regularly I rode past on my tried and true Topsy, and ogled the high-borne mare from her dainty little ears, over her radiant coat to her trim legs with hind white fetlocks but that only made me pant more yearningly. I considered various wild schemes like pretending to fall off and have Topsy turn in, or breaking a leg or anything to get me inside those tantalizing gates. Trouble was I knew Topsy would zip right past with her head and tail in the air homeward bound.

One of the first days of summer vacation I rode past as usual — or was going to ride past — until The Man himself hailed me.

"Oh, girl. Come here."

Foolish as it was I think I looked over my shoulder to see if someone had materialized behind me.

"Girl, come here."

"Me?"

"Yes, I'd like to ask a favor of you."

Now that's a switch!

"My nephew is visiting me from the city and wants to ride horseback but I'm afraid to let him ride Queen Bess. She'd be too much for him. I've seen you riding and I know you could handle her. Would you let him ride your mare as a favor to me, please, and you ride Bess until Dexter gets the hang of it?"

Stars and comets and galaxies showered down over Michigan. Skyrockets, Roman candles, sparklers, pinwheels exploded in every direction so I was too dazed to answer.

"Would you mind very much?" he prodded. "I'm sure he'd be careful and do just what you said."

I came down from Clouds Nine, Nineteen and Ninety-nine and squeaked.

"Now?"

"Sure. He can hardly wait. Got new pants and cowboy boots that're crying out to be dirtied on a horse. Come in, come in, I think he'll be in the barn brushing Queen Bess. I thought that would be safe enough, don't you agree?"

Him asking me my opinion! The glory of it.

And so My Big Day began and continued every day that week. Dex and I were fast friends from the first. A year ahead of me in school he planned to be an artist while I intended to be a writer lending a fillip to our conversations which also were leavened with his more sophisticated city ways.

Saturday we had covered Toonerville and environs from one end to the other and were dragging ourselves home, dirty and weary. As an experiment I had changed horses with him so that he was Queen Bess' consort without any problems. I had almost ridden off when he called back.

"Dot. Dot, wait a second."

Topsy and Bess knew their day's work was over and intended to tolerate no delays. Bess danced off one way and Topsy added her "pas de deux" in the other direction.

"What is it? You all right?"

"Yes, but wait up a minute. Do you want to go to the movies tonight?"

"Wha-at?" I yelled from my place down the road.

"Do you want to go to the movies tonight? It's William S. Hart, in 'Code of the West'," he bellowed.

"Oh, yes, Dex, that would be wonderful!" For the first time in my life I suddenly thought, "What'll I wear?"

X

My partnership with Topsy lasted over many years. She was just my age, so when I was in high school and college she was getting pretty long in the tooth but her spirit was undimmed, making her vulnerable to anyone who might try to "master" her without knowing what he was about.

There were no horse trailers in those days. When I wanted my horse somewhere else I had to ride her. Twice I rode her from Toonerville to Ann Arbor, a distance of around forty or so miles (depending on the route) and back again once. The last time I hitched a ride for her in a horse van going that way. Looking back I have done things *I* don't believe but know that memory must be correct.

The first time she was there through the autumn days. I had planned to ride her back on Thanksgiving Day, and I did, the little matter of a blizzard not stopping me. Toonerville was straight north so game little Tops and I faced into it the whole way. Connie on her big horse Monte rode to meet us — "came a piece" as we used to say — and it was quite a piece, but was I glad to see her looming up through the snow! And Topsy took new heart from having Monte beside her.

Of course, their presence meant that we had four long extra miles through Toonerville and on out to her farm where the mare and I rested up the next day, both of us needing a little restorative time.

The Tyrone Lyons had long since gotten tired, understandably so, of my dumping Topsy on them whenever it was not convenient for me to have her with me. My junior year I was up against it, couldn't find a haven for her anywhere, until one day Dex and I went to his uncle's new farm (he had burned out of the Toonerville home) down near Detroit.

During my visit I advanced the desirability of their having two riding horses in order that two people might ride together. When they agreed it seemed like a good idea, I was just the one to suggest the extra horse. Topsy could renew her acquaintance with Queen Bess, the Kentucky saddler.

Here again I undertook to ride Topsy from Toonerville to Dex's uncle on the Twelve Mile Road. One of the mare's most infuriating habits was being next to impossible to catch in a pasture until she was good and ready to be caught. She must have fancied herself a wild horse on the western plains but I do know there were times when if I'd had a gun I would surely have popped her one. Made me always wish to be a roper.

As a result we got a late start plus having to stop along the way at the farrier's to get her shod, making it noon or after before we really got on the road. The miles unrolled behind Topsy's energetic walk, her head swinging from side to side so that the loose reins slapped back and forth on her neck, but for each mile we covered there were two more staring at us.

Pasture-soft as she was Topsy's pizazz began to peter out before we were anywhere near our destination. Twilight was coming on and as a final complication a mean little drizzle set in. I had long since been walking to spare the old girl and before long I knew we'd never make it. Had I known where we were we'd have had a fighting chance but by that time I was lost, good and lost.

There seemed no alternative to throwing Topsy and myself onto the hospitality of someone along the way. I could put up with anything, but she was beat and needed good care, good food, and a soft stall. I considered two or three farms and discarded them as their stable facilities didn't measure up to Topsy's needs.

Finally just the right one loomed up along the road.

"They ought to have a good place for a good mare, Tops, old girl. Let's give it a try. First though, if you'll pardon me, I'll just step up on you in case of mean old dogs."

Mounting, I rode into the spacious yard surrounding a monstrous white barn, a not so monstrous house and several outbuildings. As expected a chorus of barks greeted Topsy's hoofbeats in the driveway. I headed for the backdoor which was jerked open so that a light fell on us.

"Good evening," I said pleasantly. "I am Dorothy Lyons riding my horse from Toonerville to a place on the Twelve-Mile Road, but I've lost the way, so I wondered if I could get a night's lodging for my horse and myself."

A stunned silence greeted this introduction at first — I found later that we were only about fifteen miles from the Detroit City Hall — but the man soon found his voice.

"Why, girl, we'd be glad to put you up but we ain't got anything for your horse. This place hasn't been farmed in several years."

"Thank you just the same. My mare is pretty tired and needs good care tonight. We'll just go along and find someplace else."

"Hold your horses — or one of 'em anyway. We'll jump into the pickup and go down to the next farm (same fellow owns them) and bring back enough stuff for your mare. Just get off and I'll show you where to put her 'til we're back."

While they were gone I unsaddled and rubbed the mare with a straw whisk so she was ready for the deep straw, fragrant hay and clean water provided her. They were such good people and now I don't even remember their names. Not a penny would they take for all their trouble and sent us on our way on a bright, blowy morning with good directions and good wishes.

Years later they met someone from Toonerville and recounted the experience (I suppose it was comparable to a Martian's visit).

"Oh, yeah, that would have been Babe Lyons. She rode horseback all over."

Dex's uncle was glad to get Topsy and planned all the riding he, his friends and his wife would be doing. But no one ever rides as much as planned and after a year or so he decided he couldn't keep two horses.

He gave me the bad news when Dex and I had gone down again for a day's riding, in the course of which he asked us to take a message to a neighboring farmer. The message delivered, the man cast his eyes covetously over Topsy's sleek sides, her pretty head and faultless (well, almost) conformation.

"If you ever want to sell that mare, let me know. I've taken quite a fancy to her."

"As it happens, Mr. Burnham, she'll never be for sale but I'll let you have her right now free if you promise never to sell her. Get in touch with me first."

"Oh, sure, I'd never want to sell a mare like that! She's tops."

So I left my little bay mare there and went on with all my other pressing affairs — junior year, *Junior Girls Play*, a friend's terrible accident, absorbing courses, men —and the following spring I went off to the resort where I had waited on tables two previous summers. Not long before I was due to come home a letter from Connie said "Topsy has been sold back to Toonerville. Hilda bought her out of the Detroit News classifieds but she's too much for her and she's letting any old cowboy ride her. She invited me to and when I saw her I knew it just *had* to be Topsy: I rode her past your old place and she turned in and went down around to the stable. Then I rode past Kit's and she went in and around to the pump where she always drank."

(For the long arm of coincidence that one is hard to beat: the man advertised Topsy in the Detroit News with a circulation of 500,000 and a girl in my high school class of fifteen in a town forty-five miles away bought her. I'd never dare use that in a book.)

Back in Michigan I went about getting my mare back. Under different circumstances the folks might not have let me have her at college that last fall, but they said I could. The day after my return Connie and I drove down to the Fifteen Mile Road and confronted the clod who'd sold her.

"Well, I decided I couldn't keep her any longer and I didn't know how to get in touch with you." He ignored my comment he'd had only to call Dex's uncle for my address and phone number. "Sure, I'll give the girl her money back — but I won't pay for vanning the horse out to her."

On we went to Toonerville. First a quick stop to greet Topsy and let her know her friends were on the march. The would-be cowboys had worn great bloody sores on her mouth by overbitting and raw sores on her sides from spurring her "to make her know who's boss."

Then to Hilda (Topsy wasn't stalled at her home for lack of a stable) to assert my rights and ownership of the mare. She wasn't home, however, so we decided to take Topsy down to our friend, the blacksmith to be shod since I would be riding her to Ann Arbor for the year, another 40-45 mile jaunt.

Back to Hilda's and she was home. She too was perfectly willing to let me have my property back but balked at paying the hauling fee.

"Well, I won't," I said, I hoped forcefully. "She's my property and I'm not going to pay for having her hauled all over the state. Your business is with Mr. Burnham, not me."

"If you don't pay it, you can't have the horse."

"As it just happens, I've got my horse in a place you don't know about."

"That's horse-thievin', Dorothy Lyons. I've a good notion to have you arrested."

"For stealing my own horse! Go ahead and try it."

So the Devil compounded my sins with horse stealing but there was never any mention of a lynchin'. Understandably, however, Hilda's and my relationship deteriorated to rockbottom where it is to this day. I wish I'd been a little less smartalecky but at that age such a thought would never enter your head. Now I feel quite sheepish to realize I put a $10. value on friendship.

XI

Mother once said to me, "Dorothy, never marry a man who's going to be gone five — or four — or three — days a week. You'll have more than you can handle."

(So I took her advice and never married at all.)

I do not know whether it was planned or not but our house sat by itself a-top a knoll — which was at the crown of a hill — and the nearest neighbor was three or four hundred hards away. Nevertheless, I feel sure some of our Irish brouhahas must have spanned so paltry a distance with enough force for them to know all was not peaceful with the Lyonses.

Usually when Mother went away I went with her because the climate for a vulnerable little girl was not the best. No matter what the occasion I was happy with a pencil and a pad of paper. And a good thing because many of the aging relatives were dropping off. If Mother was to show her respect and attend the funerals, there was nothing for it but that Dorothy should go too.

One minister droned on and on and on in an apparently endless parade of his fluent command of the Holy Scriptures well larded with references to the deceased. Finally even the joys of a pencil and new tablet wore thin. I tweaked Mother's skirt.

"I don't like this old funeral," I whispered when she bent down to me. She made a stern face at me and shook her head reprovingly that I should criticize the civilized ritual of a funeral. I saw I'd erred and quickly, with a demonstration of the tact I was to display throughout my life I hastened to make amends. I tweaked her skirt again.

"Don't worry, Mama. I'll like yours." But I didn't.

Of necessity Mother was just about always at the heart of the hurricane either before trying to avert disaster, during trying to mitigate its severity or afterward to bind up any wounds, be they physical or mental. One morning while I was still in grammar school I don't remember as being any more tumultous than others, the riot finally abated enough for us to get off to school — a sacred responsibility. I was the first home that afternoon and instantly on opening the door I called out,

"Mama," expecting the customary "What is it?" to which I always replied, "Nothing." All I needed was to know that Mother was there in the house. But this time — silence.

"Mama!" I tried again with a few more decibels.

Nothing. I began a quick reconnoiter of the house's twelve rooms. Still no reply to my more and more importunate cries.

By then Bob had come home and we began scouting the three acres. Still neither sight nor sound nor trail. Soon Don and Nonie came in from high school and had to do the whole routine over again. Possibly they were unconsciously stalling to put off the moment when we had to admit Mother had disappeared.

We met in solemn conclave in the kitchen — after all, first things first.

"Mama's gone," I quavered.

"Stop it, Babe. She's probably just at a friend's and was held up getting home."

Nonie as the eldest had assumed the position of command with Don her able lieutenant.

"Don, you go around to the neighbors and see if she's anywhere here. Maybe she didn't feel good and they've kept her until we got home."

"What are you going to be doing?" he asked critically, not wanting to be the only one with a job.

"I'm going to phone Mrs. Collins and Mrs. Wass and Sister Parker to see if she walked over town and was tired out."

Bob went with Don and I hung on Nonie's every word as she canvassed Mother's friends. Still no lead.

"What about Aunt Stace and Uncle Cell and all the Tyrone folks?" I asked.

"Good idea, Snooks. I'll phone them."

When all possible leads had been checked — the boys had no luck either — we met again but this time in the living room as befit the seriousness of the moment. Mother had vanished and left no trace.

In those dear, dead days the thought of foul play did not occur to any of us or our connections whom we called. Whatever had happened had to have been voluntary; Mother had absconded. I don't remember even any soul-searching on our parts. Had we contributed to her aberration? What could we have done to make parts unknown more desirable than here, home with her four lovely children and three acres to break her back on?

"What'll we do?" Bob asked, trying to keep the tremor out of his voice.

"We'll just have to phone Dad."

Each Monday morning before Dad left he wrote out his itinerary for the week with names of hotels where he could be reached. Luckily it was late in the week and he was in a nearby town, working his way home for the weekend. Rapidly checking train schedules he said he could be home in two hours on the evening train.

Nonie became the little mother and was able to pull supper together on the generous leftovers we always had. (Mother used to tell about a mean-minded neighbor when she was a little girl; she'd cook only about half enough for healthy appetites — even if thrashers were there — and when everything in sight had been eaten and the dishes polished right down to the pattern she'd look around with a laugh, "Why, we had just enough, didn't we?" It became a slogan with us if anything ran a little short.)

No one felt much like eating at first but we managed to tuck away a pretty good quantity. Bob harnessed the horse and drove down to meet Dad's train since no one but Dad could drive the car, and walking had never been his favorite activity.

By then it was pretty soon bedtime. Dad put us to bed rather awkwardly, not that any of us really needed it physically but we could do with a bit of reassurance and optimism. Dad, and therefore the whole family, had never been real long on affection or demonstrations thereof.

He sat at his desk in what we called "his" room, a misnomer of ever I heard one. The desk lamp made an island of light where he no doubt reviewed the wreckage of his marriage, the problems of four young, growing children for a travelling man, the more immediate questions facing him right now.

After several hours he heard the midnight train whistle its way into and out of Toonerville without paying much attention to it. Later, quite a lot later, for we lived well over a mile all uphill from the Grand Trunk station, feet mounted the front steps, crossed the porch and opened the front door. Dad looked up from his desk and greeted her extra brusquely from relief no doubt with the time-honored phrase that became standard with us.

"Where the hell've you been?"

"I just felt like a day in Detroit," Mother mustered all the jauntiness she could. What had seemed like a lark that morning wasn't all that cheery now.

"Well word has really gone out to the four winds that you've left us. You'll have some explaining to do." How like Dad to assume the burden was on her, not him or us or anyone but my poor, put-upon mother.

After starting school my junkets with Mother were curtailed. Sometimes a relative could come and stay; others we just had to make out by ourselves. Generally Mother was able to get back in the evening, certainly on the midnight train that was such a basic thread in Toonerville's pattern of life.

With me Bob was a real Jekyll and Hyde: one time he'd be kind and gentle like a big brother should, another the Devil took hold of him and life was a torment. When I was really small he called me Bunny and I'd comfort myself with that when the going was rough. The only reason I never killed him was I wasn't big enough, but he was small for his age and I grew fast so many times I'd think, "This time I can take him," only to get a royal drubbing to prove I was mistaken.

One time though I really scored. A Saturday morning I'd gone up to my bedroom to clean it up. The boys' room was next door and when Bob heard me he came in and began heckling.

"Don't pay any attention," I kept saying to myself. "Just don't listen to him."

That's what the folks used to tell me, but I knew he would go on, heaping indignity on indignity so I might as well explode first at last. This day I was standing at my dresser to straighten the articles while he continued plaguing me. I picked up the heavy silver hairbrush from Mother's set she let me use. I hefted it several times and whirling let it fly, knowing full well Bob would duck, and aiming about waist high.

That silver brush bounced off his scalp with the most satisfying crack I'd ever heard. Then I ran behind the bed for refuge but there was no hiding place back there.

He would undoubtedly have pulverized me but for Don who had heard it all from the next room. Rising out of bed he bounded in and grabbed Bob by the nape of the neck.

"Leave her alone, you little snipe. You've been asking for it for half an hour — she should have done it long ago."

I doubt that Mother ever knew about the confrontation on the third floor. Had she had time to notice trifles she might have seen Bob tenderly patting his crown and, taking his hand away, examining it for blood. Score one for Babe!

We were both quite small this one time Mother had gone away. He determined he was going to sleep in her big mahogany bed although she had told me I could. All through supper and evening he harassed me and kept repeating that he was going to sleep in her bed that night until I was reduced to abject tears little short of hysterics.

Finally Nonie got me aside and told me to go into

Mother's room and lock the door while they created a diversion. I made it successfully into the room, slammed the door and locked it, only to have Bob learn he had been outsmarted.

Mere wood was not made to withstand the onslaught of a furious little boy. I cowered inside while Bob pounded and banged and kicked and hammered on the offending door. Huddled in the middle of Mother's bed that even yet seems like acres of counterpane, bellering at the top of my lungs to join my voice to Bob's we needed all the distance we had from the neighbors. Bob threatened me with all the indignities and refinements of torture that a fiendish brother could devise, all of which I was sure he'd consummate.

If possible, my screams reached new highs in terror with the certainty he would make good every threat with interest.

The folk's bedroom was a big, bay-windowed room on the front of the house. Under the windows on one side was the roof over the porte cochere, or portico, at right angles to the bathroom window with the ground some twenty feet below. The big girls' room was also along the front on the other side of the bay window with a five or six foot space between there and the girls' roof.

Pausing to catch my breath I heard a scratching on the portico window. There was Don peering in and beckoning me to let him in. He had gone in and locked the bathroom door. Opening the window, he leaped from the sill across the intervening blackness to the dark, sloping roof.

Before I'd opened this window I heard a tiny tapping on the bay window. There was Nonie! She had locked her door, climbed out on the roof, poised on the edge and jumped across the black void to balance on the six-inch ledge around the bay at floor level. How she ever caught hold of anything to keep from falling back down into the lily of the valley bed, also twenty feet, I don't know as neither the window nor screen was open to afford a hold.

Bless their hearts! They didn't even think a thing of their feat, just something that had to be done to keep Babe from being scared out of her wits.

Eventually they calmed my fears, blew my nose and bedded me down. They let themselves out the door and pushed the key back under it to me. But how, I still wonder, did they unlock their doors and get back into their rooms? But neither is left to tell me.

They were a long way from saints if that seems to be the impression and weren't above taking advantage of anyone or anything to suit their wishes.

"Boy, oh boy! The circus is coming to Holly but not Toonerville," Don announced with excitement. Our towns were usually not considered worthy of even a one-night stand.

From then on all thoughts and plans hinged on getting to see the circus. Bob had a paper route too, making two large, very large, obstacles to their attendance.

"It's really no problem," Nonie pointed out at the last minute. "Snooks is too little to go to the circus, so she can deliver your papers."

Judging by my attachment to an express wagon, small size, I couldn't have been more than six or seven - eight? Too small to go to the circus but not too small to deliver two paper routes! Despite my most impassioned refusal, they would not take "no" or even "I don't want to" for an answer. Instead they piled into somebody's auto and departed. Bob even had the nerve to call back to me.

"Don't forget Miss Elkins' has to go into that jardiniere on her porch."

"Better get started for the depot, Babe. Train'll be in pretty soon," Don yelled. The fast afternoon train didn't stop at Toonerville but bundles of papers were thrown off for the paper boys.

I was already in tears before I started and the rank injustice, the inhumanity of it, compounded my tears. Pulling my little express wagon I sorted around and found the two bundles for Bob and Don. Then my misery was trebled, quadrupled. Each bundle was tied in hard knots with rope strong enough to be hurled from a moving train. There I was in my blue gingham dress, no pockets, no nothing, nothing that would ever open those stacks.

My sobs reached a crescendo; tears closed my eyes, but like an obedient old horse I set out on the route I knew. Good fortune was with me or I might never have gotten the packs open.

My first stop was the Ten Cent Barn Livery Stable and a nice man tipped back in a chair out in front was moved by the violence, if not the noise, of my woe.

"Come on now, sis. It can't be all that bad. What's the trouble?" he asked kindly.

All the frustration, the wild rebellion, the bitterness that I was not big enough to go with them to Holly *but* big enough to keep them in the good graces of their customers boiled out. And on top of that, I'd never be able to get the packets undone anyway.

"Well, now, just you dry your eyes, sugar. I've got a good sharp knife here that'll cut that rope. You can give me my paper and before you know it they'll all be delivered."

His soothing words and kindly manner did much to quiet my bellering and get me lined out. Both bunches of The Detroit News were duly parceled out to the correct subscribers and I went home, an embittered child. I wonder how a child psychologist would have interpreted what that experience did to my psyche or my id or whatever's the word these days? All I know is it made me a little warier of siblings' schemes.

Bob and I were cat-and-dog all through school, high school and into college. Luckily our paths didn't cross quite so often as everyone's interests broadened. Then one day Bob got engaged to a nice girl, one I liked and one who liked me. She was at the house one day we were bickering back and forth.

"Why don't you kids grow up?" she asked. "You're supposed to be mature, sensible adults — almost."

"I'd be happy to if Bob would leave me alone. He's always the one who picks the fight."

"It takes two to make a fight," she countered glibly.

"But not to start it. I'm not going to lie down and let him walk all over me. Why, when I was little I used to think 'maybe I'm illegitimate; that's probably why things are so tough' but then I'd think, 'No, I can't be. I'm the youngest.'"

(Up to that time my reading had not included adultery, only prenuptial flings.)

Both Bob and Ruth began scoffing at "poor little me" until Mother intervened.

"Gracious, Dorothy! Don't ever let Dan know I told you, but he didn't want another child." She told how he'd thought three were enough.

Whether it was that or whether Bob had just fallen into a pattern that, once broken, never returned, I don't know. But from that day he did an about face and we've been the best of friends ever since. How different — well, no matter.

XII

Weather and its changing patterns are vitally important to an outdoors person, and so I accumulated old weather sayings and saws to supplement the feeble U.S. Weather Service when I was growing up. They might have had little force in some other climate pattern but in the zone of "prevailing westerlies" the weather marched right across the continent from the Pacific to the Atlantic — with occasional aberrations which only served to make talking about the weather interesting.

One loveliest of lovely Saturday mornings brother Bob was mowing the lawn and I was frogging around, being no help, only another presence. The green, fragrant blades lay on the barbered lawn, enough to make any nose twitch with delight be it rabbit or horse or homo sapiens.

For a time I contented myself with making little haycocks.

"Don't leave them there or they'll mildew and burn a patch in the grass," Bob cautioned with his maddening big-brotherly air.

"I'm not! D'ya think I'm a city slicker?"

Interrupted in my play I rolled over on my back and stared up at the bluest blue any artist ever dared paint. I sat up to check. Nope. Not a cloud in the sky.

"Hmmm," I mused professionally. "Apt to be a storm in a day or two."

"Whaaat did you say?" Bob could not believe his ears. He too swiveled around to check the unbroken blueness. Further comment became jeers.

"Apt to be a storm in a few days. 'A deep, clear sky of fleckless blue breeds a storm in a day or two,' " I quoted glibly.

Bob didn't let me forget my impromptu forecast then or later. At lunch (which we always called dinner) he said during a lull.

"Better be careful for a few days, folks. Babe says there's going to be a storm."

Everyone's reaction was the same open-mouthed astonishment and hilarity Bob had greeted my off-hand statement with, so he attempted to milk it for all it was worth. By then the conversation had swirled on to other topics. Later when he went to town, however, he played for another coup in the barbershop.

"Better tell everyone to carry their umbrellas. Babe says there's going to be a storm."

That was greeted with such hilarity in the face of one of Michigan's most breath-takingly beautiful days he didn't let it die there until my reputation as a weather prophet — even as a rational human being — ebbed to less than zero.

"If I could only learn to keep my mouth shut," I thought for the hundredth time.

So two days later had I even seen a funnel cloud

heading for us I might have kept silent. Certainly a black little whiff that blew up over the horizon was not worthy of comment. Of course, it kept getting bigger and blacker but lots of times they did.

When the blackness became tinged with copper and kind of a shiny gun metal people opined there might be a storm. When treetops suddenly bent nearly double and the air was filled with flying bits housewives rushed to close windows and get clothes off the lines; farmers unhitched their teams and raced for their barns; even the unwariest took cover.

With a whosh and a bang the storm hit: rain like a solid curtain, then the staccato rattle of hailstones that cut the local crops to ribbons within three minutes, the worst hailstorm to hit Toonerville in years.

On such small coincidences are reputations born.

But I didn't quit while I was ahead. No, not me, not so long as my grandfather was Patrick Vincent O'Lyons. I bided my time and another gorgeous day rolled around when I expressed the opinion it was going to rain. Just possibly I had been overplaying my earlier triumph and Dad decided I needed taking down.

"Nonsense. Don't let one success go to your head, Dorothy."

"Well, it's going to, I betcha." This latter was a figure of speech which Dad picked up.

"How much?"

I hadn't really intended to put my money where my mouth was but backed into a corner I still wouldn't give in. A nickel was the most I'd ever bet, indeed that was pretty big money then.

"A dime," I said with a jaunty air.

When the details were complete it would have to rain before midnight for me to collect or forfeit my allowance. That too was a Saturday and while I was still solvent Kit and I went to the movie to see the latest Tom Mix. On leaving the movie palace I was overjoyed to see storm clouds gathering.

No one concentrated harder than I on building them up, and as we reached home at 11:30 the first spats of rain began falling. Mother and Dad were both in bed and deeply asleep but did that deter me? Not one instant. I banged on their door and yelled, "It's raining, Dad! You owe me a dime."

Dad's reply has been expurgated.

XIII

I began life as a Presbyterian where I attended Sunday School in a fairly haphazard fashion until I was six or seven. Perhaps the thing that queered formal religion for me was lemon meringue pie, Mother's lemon pie. I was the only one sent off on a Sunday a.m. while the infidels lolled at home.

Sunday dinner began about half an hour before I got out, my soul safe for another week, so by the time I had trudged a mile home all, and I mean every crumb, of Mother's ineffable lemon meringue pie had been licked up. How could concern about my afterlife stand up against that? Occasional absences became more and more frequent until I no longer went at all.

Mother was always a devout Christian with a questing spirit that sought the Key to it all. It was during the family's two-year stay in Chicago that a little known sect called the Bible Students caught her attention. From that moment on she felt she had found the Way, the Truth and the Light.

Unlike some religious people, however, she lived it as much as a demanding family permitted and was truly a practicing Christian. "I was hungry and ye fed Me." No person ever left our door hungry nor did anyone suffer for lack of shelter and nursing or any kind of care that could lift them up and help them in any way.

The waifs and strays who became a part of our family were accepted by us children as a way of life. In retrospect it hardly seems fair that Mother got all the credit for her good works when it was Dad who brought in the wherewithal. One after another he bore with what passed for good grace however he may have felt about it.

Only one I remember he blackballed unequivocally, a toothless old lady whose relatives had flimflammed her out of her money and then put her in the poorhouse (a reality in those days). Being able-bodied someone else took her out of there and home with them to work for her keep but weren't good to her . . . she may have been a little light in the head.

Somehow her story got onto Mother's grapevine and she became an avenging angel, not resting until old Mary was a resident of the Lyons household. She was inoffensive enough in many ways and tried really very hard to be a good family member — for instance, when using her knife to get butter from the butter plate she carefully cleaned it from hilt to tip on each side — with her tongue.

I believe Dad's words in his ultimatum amounted to "It's Mary or me" though I am certain he never said anything in as few words. There were a couple of other wraiths Mother tried valiantly to rehabilitate but got nowhere, due mostly to a lack of cooperation from the parties of the first part.

One who just about qualifies as a family member was Louise, Weezie to me, only child of Mother's older sister who died during my fourth summer. She was staying with another sister, Aunt Ada, during her final illness, since Uncle Jim was off somewhere chasing Lady Luck. I clearly remember the urgent phone call, frantic harnessing of Old Doc and the trip up there, Mother and someone else, possibly Grandma, in front and another child (possibly Louise) sitting in the boot with me. Curiously, I have no recollection of fast driving. Looking back it seems as though Doc just took his own gait — but left to his decision that could have been pretty fast. Nowadays people would hardly think it suitable, but we two small ones filed into the bedchamber with other relatives of the dying woman.

Uncle Jim was such a soldier of fortune he was seldom home, but wherever he went he took his "black cat" with him, for he was a born loser. While in the Alaskan gold fields he was down at the bottom of a deep hole working his claim late in the afternoon when the waning light glinted off the sought for gold. He dug feverishly into the gravelly earth to uncover a vein of gold, rich beyond belief. After a lifetime of disappointments he could hardly believe his eyes!

Sample after sample he dug out to reassure himself. By now it was almost dark, so he exuberantly decided to sleep and savor his good luck overnight before really beginning to mine it in earnest. In his exhilaration he scarely noticed a trickle of water that oozed from the hole the samples had come from.

He never slept a wink until the early hours after planning all that he would do with his unaccustomed wealth: Louise would go to a good school; Aunt Hattie should have the prettiest dresses, the best help he could find; Floyd, son of his previous marriage who accompanied him on many of his travels would have good, warm clothes and never go hungry again.

At last he went to sleep with the smile still on his face. Waking, he took time for only the quickest meals before hurrying off to the diggings. Strong man that he was, he broke down in sobs when he saw the richest claim he had ever had: that tiny trickle of water must have built up and, draining into his excavation hour by hour all night, filled it to the brim. Miles and miles from any railroad or transportation the mine would have had to be pure gold to pay for hauling pumps and other equipment in there — and there was only his word and opinion as to how rich it really was!

But that had been years earlier. After Aunt Hattie's death Louise came to live with us. She was a plain girl but the lively expressions that flitted across her face relieved its plainness. Nothing could be done about her hair, however. It was that baby fine texture no hairdresser's art could make do anything it did not want to, and that was be itself, fine and soft as cornsilk. Cut it was short fuzz; grown out it was long fuzz.

Louise was warmhearted and craved affection which was hard in so busy and diffuse a family as ours though she couldn't help feeling the unspoken love there. Nonie and she were about the same age and shared the "girls' room." They were as unlike as oil and water which brought on many stormy scenes. Nonie always accused Mother of favoring Louise, and maybe she did in an effort to be fair to the motherless girl. I was enough younger to move in a different world; as I grew older our age gap was not so noticeable and we had many good times together though I did understand some of Nonie's problems.

Once she was going to tell me a joke but forgot. "It's real funny," she assured me and began to laugh. Soon we both went into gales of laughter at the joke she couldn't remember. (A young lady went into a florist's asking for some "salivas — and there's something else I was supposed to get. I wonder —" "Maybe spitunias, madam.")

Weezie was a piano player to set your feet tapping and I adored her for it. I would follow her around, begging her to play this or that. Once she turned to the back page with the publisher's name, etc. and played the print instead of music and I was enthralled.

During her senior year in her search for love she eloped with her high school sweetheart. Neither was really ready for marriage but they did manage to make a go of it until economic factors threw sand in the oil. From there she had her ups and downs. Mother rejoiced during the former and brought her home to Toonerville to build her up for her next tilt at windmills.

Happily she later married a good man who made her last years happy and comparatively prosperous. With a boost from here and there they acquired a good, small hotel along the ocean front in a thriving town, an occupation that was perfect for her open, cheery nature, so people kept returning again and again.

From time to time we had other relatives stay with us during periods of personal crisis. Two of the Adams boys were long term visitors, Dan to finish high school after his father threw him out, and Dick just because he wanted to, I guess.

Dan had more than his share of braggadocio and was always colliding with his father's temper. An example of his bluster was one day the boys were riding along a Detroit street with Dan driving the Model T. In turning a corner a streetcar nearly sideswiped the T as Dan hadn't given any ground to allow for the sweeping rear end. This got his dander up more than somewhat.

"The damn fool. I should've hit him," he growled as though he were driving a tank.

Both Dan and Dick were a great help to Mother in the kitchen. They had had no sisters until the three boys were grown up, so they had to help their own mother, Aunt Molly.

While Dan was big Dick was little. Having been a sickly baby he never matched the physiques of his father and brothers but he had a ready wit which coupled with a dry delivery assured his popularity.

Another family member after we moved to Ann Arbor was Guy Miller, a Fenton D.P. After his father died his mother was employed as matron in a nurses' dorm at the University where Guy obviously couldn't live. Until we moved to town he had just been a boy living in a college rooming house but he gladly sank back into our cushion of friendship and togetherness.

During my undergraduate days an auto ban was instituted but being a "town girl" I didn't abide by it as strictly as some. One night Guy and I went to a basketball game in the field house and Dad said "take the car." Great, until a day or two later I received a summons from the Dean of Students inquiring as to how our Hudson had been observed parked outside the Field House.

"My friend, Guy Miller, was the driver. He lives with us."

"Isn't that a bit unusual, letting a non-family member take the car?"

"I don't see why. As I say he lives there, and if none of the men is home and the furnace needs attention, Guy goes down to it. Or if Mother has an errand and no one to run it, Guy does it. Isn't taking the car only returning a favor?"

"And you weren't there?"

"Of course, I was. Wouldn't it have been silly to walk if our own car was going?"

The dean wasn't convinced but actually didn't have a case. Lucky me!

The boys always teased Guy about his name. He had a stammer, and for someone with that problem Guy Miller was as hard a combination to say as could be dreamed up. However, M-m-miller was easier to get going on than G-g-g-g-g, so he always said when asked his name, "MMiller—Guy-Miller."

For our last two years in college Connie came to live with us too. Between the boys and their friends and us and our friends it seemed like a constant houseparty.

Our family has always been great games lovers and once we learned to play bridge we were hooked. Many a weekend we'd start playing after breakfast and, with suitable pauses for creature comforts, continue until well past bedtime. Then that wasn't enough, so we began arranging our class schedules to allow two or three hours for noon games. Of course, our grades weren't all that good that semester.

Then there was Fred. He had gone by the time we moved to Ann Arbor but if the story of his life were written the Lyonses would loom pretty large. Mother's good works did not stop there, for she truly lived her faith, every hour of every day.

Their beliefs were not heralded with much fanfare but

hit a responsive chord in many people, especially the lowly and humble and troubled and beset. A better life right here was what they sought. No heaven with golden streets and pearly gates but a resurrection to bring their dear ones back to live on a perfect earth.

Before that, however, there is to be a great time of trouble such as no man has even seen. According to a timetable worked out from the Bible it was to begin in 1914. We were in Toonerville by then with Mother taking it all to her heart.

The cupboards in our pantry did not go clear to the ceiling and the lofty ceilings left a three or four foot gap. Time of Trouble or not, Mother was going to look after her family. In 1913 or early 1914 that space was packed with hundred-weights of flour and sugar, bags of salt, coffee beans and some odds and ends she thought would come in handy. There was no way to disguise the stocks and word soon flew around that Mrs. Lyons was ready for heavy weather.

Dad was a consummate tease, not just an unimaginative twit, so he could embroider it into conversation in a dozen different ways, but it never ruffled Mother's serenity. Yet when 1914 brought WW I, sugar rationing and other shortages I don't recall Dad ever eating his words, publicly anyway, but he should have for he was a man who had to have two *loaded* spoonsful of sugar in strong coffee akin to lye.

These supplies were gradually used up when nothing worse developed, but who's to say the Great Time of Trouble did not begin then? It seems to me we might well be in the Prologue right now.

Once I asked, "What kind of trouble, Mother — wars, plagues, what?"

"I think every kind, Dorothy, including anarchy, civil strife, natural disasters."

Many times in the past few years I've thought of her words. Riots, hostages, skyjacking, what are any of them but anarchy? And I wonder uneasily what a lack of water could do to us and all those earthquakes! Billy Graham and other religious leaders also expect this time of trouble foretold in Revelations which only the good will survive which adds "Millions now living will never die" to the "Millions now dead will live again."

Many years ago their leaders changed the name to Jehovah's Witnesses, based on some Bible passage. Since then they have met with bitter criticism, even hatred, why I never understood. When I knew them as a child they were all good, gentle, sincere folks living by their faith. In those days, possibly now too, there were "pilgrims" who went forth to spread the Word. As a rule they were from humble stations in life, generally poor but sufficiently dedicated to pay their own way — or at least to supplement whatever rockbottom expenses they received. Of course, they were entertained by one of the faithful, but it was always Mrs. Lyons.

One dear old man missed his connection at the train terminal so arriving at midnight had had no dinner. He said to Mother apologetically.

"I was so hungry I bought a nickel's worth of peanut brittle. Sister Lyons, do you think that was too worldly of me?"

Her Faith was so personal and immediate Jesus walked at her elbow all day long. I surely hope she is up There now, helping to get ready for company.

XIV

Brother Don was probably the most soft-hearted of the family — or maybe it showed up more. Once he said to me, "Babe, I wouldn't mind crying in movies if I didn't sob out loud."

Mother rarely made the rounds of us kids at bedtime to "tuck us in" and kiss us goodnight. Instead we went to her for a kiss and a snuggle and a confidence if need be. One night she thought Don was unusually upset about something, so she spent extra time with him. Finally it came out in a rush of tears and cries.

"Oh, Mother, there's been this poor kid in my class. An orphan the Winchesters got out of the orphanage to work for them. I knew from the way he acted in school they didn't treat him right. But today he told me he'd run away."

Mother made soothing sounds calculated to make Don know she was with him.

"He doesn't have any place to sleep tonight. Told me he was going to cover up with the fallen leaves in that ditch up the road. But, Mother, it's October. He'll freeze to death — even if he *is* used to being miserable. Can't I go get him, Mother? Please, please!"

Always a champion of the underdog Mother was ready to charge into battle with flags flying and trumpets sounding. Dad was home that night, however, and his more cautious nature precluded bringing Fred into our home, a deliberate insult to the Winchesters, but he also had a wonderfully Machiavellian mind.

"No, you can't bring him home, Donald, but there's nothing to say you couldn't take him something hot to eat — if your mother could whip it up — and send him to our hayloft where, with a couple of blankets he could be quite comfortable. Or even downstairs in the extra stall next to the horse would be quite warm."

The Lyons family was committed. From then on it was a legal battle with Fred, his person and his well being in the balance. Turned out he had been taken from the orphanage, housed in a flimsy shed on the backporch, fed on leftovers, clothed from cast-offs, and accorded not one shred of consideration or affection.

Not that he was used to any. A foundling with no notion of his antecedents he had been reared at the orphanage until this fine, Christian couple, motivated by the Devil, offered to take him into their home.

I've no idea what steps and legal moves were involved, but at last Dad was declared Fred's guardian and he came to live with us. Whatever his parentage, they must have been big because at fifteen Fred was well on the way to being a big, big man. Also, it was conjectured that he had an Indian strain because of his swarthy complexion with good red blood coloring his cheeks. And one day after a light snow Fred's tracks to the barn were as ding-toed as Hiawatha's. He went to school with the rest of us and did very well while at athletics he was almost another Jim Thorpe.

Time went on with Fred fitting into the family picture with little difficulty except that any deviltry my brothers couldn't think up, Fred could.

The big bonus point was that now Mother had real help, not just a pack of no-good kids. Fred's background had trained him in all phases of housework and his gratitude was so ever-renewing he'd have done anything including walking through fire for Mother.

One weekend Connie was going to stay overnight with me for some reason, a real treat, as her value as an extra hand made any kind of absence difficult. From her air of suppressed excitement all day in school I knew she had something up her sleeve, but I was not prepared for the real glory of it.

"Up her sleeve" figuratively, in the best western tradition was a gun, all shiny and beautiful. Made of cast metal it was little more than a cap pistol, but it fired blank cartridges (or "ca'tridges" as we called them) with such a satisfactory report it couldn't be told from the real thing.

We tramped up Denton Hill, one of our favorite stamping grounds. At first we hid behind a ridge of gravel along the road and played Indians attacking stagecoach. This, however, did not last long and we quickly reverted to the twentieth century, for every report made cars skid to a halt, a worried driver jump out and circle his vehicle, and finding no blowout, he would scratch his head and drive on.

Tiring of this anonymous game (we daren't jump out and claim credit for the incident) we went back to my place for awhile.

"Let's go show, Kit," I suggested. The street was a right-angled route; we used to take the hypotenuse crosslots until this new neighbor forbade our crossing his property. Living right at the corner Sam's was a strategic location.

"Look, old Sam and his wife are sitting on the lawn," I whispered. "Let's fire as often as we can going past there." Anything to ruffle this unpoular citizen's feelings.

No soldiers in Custer's command could have done a better "rapid fire" than we did and though we were on the sidewalk within a few feet of the two they didn't seem to hear us.

Until on the way back, after making sure Kit was suitably impressed. Walking along the sidewalk we noted that Mrs. Sam was no longer visible but Sam was! He bore down on us with the fury of an avenging angel. His six-two frame quivered with barely controlled anger, his eyes glinted like daggers, his mustache quivered with fierceness.

"I ought to horsewhip you, you unspeakable little savage. You've shocked my wife into a nervous breakdown. I've had to put her to bed — and all because of your undisciplined savagery."

This attack directed solely at me so took my breath away I spoke not one word in self-defense.

"Did his eyes glow red to you?" I asked Connie afterward.

"I was too scared to look at him!"

Arriving home we poured out the story to Bob and Fred who had returned during our absence. And here let me explain that Sam was a close friend of the Winchesters, one who had helped them with their problems of disciplining Fred whose regard for Sam was lower than Salton Sea.

"Give the gun to us. We'll walk by firing, and see what he says to people as big as he is."

Turned out Sam said nary a word, in fact he didn't

even show his ugly face. And so what was working up to a neighborhood feud petered out. We thought.

The incident was soon forgotten when I learned that a Girl Scout camp had been established on Lobdell Lake. It was a Detroit-based organization and sounded alluring beyond possible reality.

I was never a joiner but did like the camaraderie of people. I had read every book in the library, boys' or girls' about school and camp life, team happenings even just groups of friends, but in such a small town had had no chance to experience any of it. And here practically right in my back yard was the embodiment of The Rover Boys — Motor Girls — Trilby this and Betsy that.

From discreet inquiry I learned that Lobdell Lake was anywhere from fifteen to twenty-five miles from Toonerville. No problem. One Saturday morning I saddled Topsy bright and early and set out. How I eventually reached my goal I'll never know as road maps were few and prized, but arrive I did.

Riding into the gate where a sign announced it was Camp Something-or-Other I introduced myself to the first person to appear. I suppose it was a good deal like someone from outer space strolling into camp and saying "hello" in an intelligible language.

I'm sure I was just as much an oddity: real riding apparel had not reached Toonerville, nice girls didn't wear boys' pants, so I wore the only other divided-leg garment available, black sateen gym bloomers; short whitey/blonde hair and blue eyes no doubt accentuated by a sunburn (I never tanned); I hope my middy was clean but wouldn't put any money on it; and a manner as friendly and ingratiating as a stray puppy's.

As luck would have it some girls were working on their Horsemanship Merit Badge — (without a horse within miles) so my information and misinformation were eagerly sought. The leaders decided I could do little harm and might acquaint their charges with a sidelight on American culture so were very cordial, winning my heart completely by inviting me to lunch.

Some girls were there for just a week, others for two, and much of the conversation revolved around that second week. Wednesday, its middle day, there was to be a day-long canoe trip (with Michigan's chain of lakes that would be no problem). And, thrill beyond thrill, I was invited to join them for that second week even if I didn't live in Detroit!

"Thank you so much, it's very nice of you, I'd like to very much," I chittered, all the time wondering how I'd ever get the required $25. tuition. However, I took the necessary information and promised to let them know if I would be there. "Well, I'd better be getting on. Topsy and I have a ways to go."

"Have you far to go?" one leader asked, thinking I was from a neighboring farm.

"No, not bad, only over to Toonerville."

"Toonerville! Why that's miles and miles."

"Yes, it's a ways, but we made it over. We'll make it back."

"But you can't possibly be home by dark. Maybe you ought to stay."

"Oh, no, thanks. There's a good moon tonight and I know our way."

Swinging into the saddle as jauntily as any western hero I rode out through the magic gateway. All the way home I was practicing various approaches to Mother to make her say "yes" to such an outlandish request. I hit on just the right one though, whatever it was, and she consented (where, I wonder did she ever dig up that $25. from?)

The intervening days crept past as imperceptibly as a caterpillar on a slippery surface. When all but two had elapsed, the ultimate in catastrophies occurred.

A deputy sheriff drove in the yard in a blue car, and served Mother (in Dad's absence) with a summons to appear in court in Flint with the girl child known as Dorothy to answer charges that she did with malice and aforethought shoot the patient, inoffending wife of one Samuel Dean on the such and such day — For months I felt sick to my stomach if a strange car drove in the yard and if it was blue a walloping headache hit me.

Mine was never a flighty nature, but I came as close to hysterics that day as I'll probably ever come.

"My camp! My canoe trip! What'll they think? Oh, Mama, that mean old man! I'd like to kill him. He's a real-life Devil."

"Now, Dorothy, just hush up and never say anything like that again. I agree with you, he's not a nice man, but just calm down and let's think this over."

"There's nothing to think over. He's ruined my vacation. He's —"

"No, now maybe he hasn't. Courts take a long time. Chances are it'll never be called that soon. You can just go along to your camp and on the odd chance your case is going to come up I'll send Rolland for you —"

"But what'll I say? How can I tell them?"

"He'll just say your mother is sick and you have to go home — and hopefully you'll be back in a day or two."

It was left that way. I packed for camp with as mixed emotions as Jack The Ripper if he'd been going for an outing on the Thames before his sentencing. I arrived and joined in their merry games, I guess, but of the first few days I remember not one thing. Not until Tuesday afternoon the night before the canoe trip.

A cloud of dust heralded the approach of the bakery truck Bob's good friend Brownie drove. As arranged Bob declared Mother was sick and I was needed at home.

"Supper is all ready, Dorothy dear. Better stay and have a bite to eat before you go."

That was the last thing I wanted but they were all so genuinely sympathetic in the face of my terrible distress each one tried to comfort me with some tasty morsel. Never as long as memory remains will I forget trying to choke down those mashed potatoes, yellowed with plenty of butter and tastefully garnished with chopped parsley.

At last we were able to leave. There was no room in the driver's compartment, so I had to ride in the panel body with the bakery trays, a fitting tumbril for a condemned person.

Word had come in from Connie that the gun had been confiscated as evidence, an ominous note. Recollection does not extend to our preparations of which I am sure there were many, Mother being adamant that her ewe lamb would be clean and neat.

All I remember is walking into the courtroom, a grim, depressing chamber in those days. Nor did juveniles have a court of their own! We were sitting on the same benches with the prostitutes, drunks, thieves, and probably murderers. One pretty young woman looked down at me and said,

"Goodness, dearie, looks like we're starting younger and younger."

I thought she was nice but Mother jerked me away to another bench. The judge must have had a little girl at home because my case was called very early, far out of numerical order surely.

Mother and I and the lawyer arose, walked through the little gate and faced His Honor while the clerk read the heinous details of the People vs Dorothy Lyons.

"Let me see Exhibit A," he said. Soberly the clerk (or somebody) handed the little pistol up to him. Almost before it was in his hands, his jaw dropped and widened in the heartiest laugh that courtroom had heard in many a day. People in the corridors looked astonished at this foreign sound.

"Case dismissed!" His roar could have been heard in the basement. "What poppycock! What damned nonsense! What is happening to our judicial system if we have to prosecute babies?"

Mother must have felt relieved. I didn't. Dismissed or not, I had missed the all-day canoe trip, the highlight of the week. Back at camp I had to suffer hearing all the details, how so-and-so lost her shoe and it floated away, and on and on. Many fine things have happened to me since but never an all-day canoe trip on Lobdell Lake.

XV

That we thought was that. Not so! Sam's next move was to have the folks served with "show cause" papers to take me away from them as unmanageable, and committed to a reform school, the exact charges being that "she rides horseback, wears bloomers and a white bulldog follows her."

One able lawyer Clarence S. Tinker, was another law school friend of Dad's. He must have made a pretty good thing off the Lyonses when even the baby furnished him with a nice fat case, two if you count the separate actions. Sam we could understand, sort of, but why would the other presumably reputable lawyer stoop to drawing up the charges in such a ridiculous case? With Tinker's urging the case was thrown out unequivocally.

As the years passed it almost began to seem unreal to me until fairly recently a cousin said, "I was always friends with that lawyer's girls in school, but I never felt the same about them again."

So it wasn't a dream, but Sam must surely have been listening to the Devil to have carried a small-town feud to such lengths. One bright spot, however, he never had any children of his own.

From then on Fred was the whipping boy for anything that went wrong in town be it serious or trivial. And he was an obsession with Sam. Fred could be walking along the street and if Sam drove past in his buggy he'd jump out, cursing like a pirate, and chase Fred with the buggy whip. Never caught him, of course, and lucky for him for what sixty-year-old man could tangle with a young Jim Thorpe.

This went on for some time, Sam vowing to give Fred the thrashing of his life but never quite catching him.

Until the day Sam was in the bus station. He'd seen Fred go along the street and began telling everyone all the things he'd do if he ever caught him.

As he finished his diatribe well larded with words that don't belong here, Fred unsuspectingly walked in the side door. Put-up-or-shut-up time.

"Now I've got you, you lowdown scum, nothing better than a common criminal. I'll give you what you've deserved for years."

The last words were half lost as with a roar Sam went for Fred. The latter would never have attacked an old man, but an old man coming at you with murder in his heart and destruction in his hands was something else. Sam landed his first and only punch on Fred before retribution caught up with him.

One — two — three! Both Sam's eyes were blackened, his nose bloodied. He staggered backward against the wall where coats were hung in cold weather. In hot weather the hooks were just right for displaying a man. Fred effortlessly picked up Sam's six-two frame and hooked his torn shirt on a hook.

Ducking out the side door again before those in the bus station had caught their breaths, Fred saw our Model T and knew Don was near. And so Fred left Toonerville, Don taking him down near Pontiac where he'd heard of a job opening.

"Give a dog a bad name," however, and everything will be blamed on him. Shortly after that a local belle learned to her dismay that she was pregnant. She had no hesitation in naming Fred as the father.

Once more Don to the rescue. Racing down to Pontiac in order to beat the sheriff there, Don snatched Fred from his room.

"You'll have to enlist to get away from here, Weasel. (His last name was Weiss which, of course, became Weasel.) "They can't find you there. Write as soon as you know where you're going."

Where he went was France, the forerunner of many

thousands, hundreds of thousands, more. I remember April 6, 1917 vividly: Dad stood in the middle of the kitchen unfolding the paper with its black six-inch headline — WAR DECLARED. Mother's expression must have been "I told you so" or hers was a stronger nature than mine. Had I been older World War I would have had much more impact on me. Nonie was Miss War Worker of 1917 with her diverse patriotic activities but my sole contribution to the effort was taking my money to school to buy War Stamps.

The next electrifying event was our mill burning. Nonie and I sat on the back steps in the chill, before dawn air and watched the sky light up, being very sure it was "those Germans who set it on fire." Without really understanding what the news in the paper meant I sorrowed when it was bad and the folks had long faces and rejoiced at Allied victories as reflected in their expressions and table conversation.

The only other local citizen's reaction that I can recall was a poor, dim-witted lad, who he was or where he lived I don't know now. The major event, war with Germany, had penetrated his confused head and he resolved to do his bit. Every morning, rain or snow or shine, he dressed and walked to the outskirts of town, any outskirts, and set up his vigil for the day in order to warn the townspeople if the Germans were coming.

Don was only sixteen but a big, strapping sixteen that could work an older person off his feet. With Fred in the service he chafed at his inability to go. One day when he and a friend were in Detroit the pressure could not be denied. They enlisted in the Navy, lying about their ages. I think Don really thought Dad would not permit it and get him out as under age. Dad, however, may have thought that possibly the Navy would succeed in making a man of his overgrown boy, who too often seemed to consort with the Devil.

"No, no, if the Navy is what you want I'll not stand in the way. Good luck."

Without knowing one thing about it I feel almost sure there must have been a confrontation between Mother and Dad that he would permit her first boy to go off to war without raising a finger to save him. Or she may have felt the same way. Don and his cronies had been in one scrape after another, some harmless, some not so. The Navy could have looked like a good solution.

I was heartbroken, proud, fearful, elated, frightened, hopeful by turns and carried the Brownie box camera he gave me the night before he went away like a talisman. Great Lakes Naval Training Station was the natural base for a Michigan recruit, the distance from Detroit to Chicago from home. He was a mighty homesick laddie at first away from home and Mother's cooking. The first thing he did on his first furlough was go to the henhouse, gather one dozen eggs, break them into a greased fry pan and gobble them down like an appetizer.

He finished boot training (if it was called that then) and whatever else was expected. Then word came his outfit was going to be shipped out. Our flivver was still fairly new, leading Mother and Nonie to connive on a tour to Great Lakes. They kept it secret from Dad until they just had to tell him since he would be driving. As expected he blew his cork.

"Of all the harebrained ideas to think five of us could drive across Michigan in that heap of tin. Where'd we stay when we got there? What about food? What about leaving the house?" Mother or Nonie had answers ready for each objection.

"Well, well — when do you think we ought to leave?" Dad backed down rarely but then with grace.

Not much of that trip comes to mind except the broadest of broad smiles with which Don answered his summons to the hospitality house as he hadn't been told we were coming in case we didn't make it.

Dad was right. The Navy did make a big difference in Don and his mind matured to catch up with his body. Important to me, as one of the home folks his thoughts had turned back to, little sister became something to be cherished.

My most vivid recollection is Armistice Day. Schools, stores, offices, everything closed and we all converged on the main street, at first just a howling, yelling, singing, cheering, crying mob. Someway someone marshalled us into a parade that was the happiest, craziest parade Toonerville ever saw or ever would see.

The high spot to me was a stately, sedate spinster who turned all her clothes backwards, including her bushy fox stole. Wearing it around her waist with the foxtail bouncing along in back, she wardanced down the street. Not too much later she became engaged and married a very quiet type, local opinion having it that he had been smitten by her joyous spontaneity.

The "war to end war" was over and everyone was unreservedly happy with no thought of the monumental problems that lay ahead. And rightly so. Omar said "best trust the happy moments."

With the arrival of peace the Lyons' big problem was getting Don out of the service (despite his enlistment for "the duration" which meant little) without waiting for bureaucracy to take its ponderous course. School was waiting for Don and, of course, he was panting with impatience. Once again Dad's law school friend in Congress put in a few words in the right places and presto! Don was home.

He had never been shipped out, having gotten as far as Newport News, Virginia before the Armistice, so was luckier than Fred who saw service in Europe. His homecoming was much later and, in fact, he never came back to Toonerville although his name had been cleared. Long before the Armistice, in time to make the belle an "honest woman" a stay-at-homer had admitted paternity and married her. Fred settled in Detroit, married not long afterward, and set about becoming a pillar of the community.

XVI

"Dorothy, jump on Topsy and go down to the Busy Bee for a loaf of bread. I just didn't have time to bake yesterday and we're all out. Your father will be mad as a wet hen at dinner. Yes, I suppose you can get some candy," she answered my unspoken question.

I flew through my minimal preparations and set out at a brisk trot through the morning sunlight. Saturday, the first day of spring vacation, perfect weather, candy — what more could mortal want!

From habit Topsy stopped at the hitching post outside the south side's busiest emporium (just as the name implied). A quick wrap around the post and I hurried inside to savor an always-astonishing array of goods: groceries, of course, from home-cured ham and bacon through luxury items such as scented soaps on into what at the time seemed like Oriental opulence in ladies' garments, a little hardware, some basic drugs, a few sewing supplies "in case" rounded off by just a tad of harness requirements such as a few snaps, long and short straps, and some celluloid rings to dress up the display.

But it was the homely, day-to-day grocery stock that endeared the store to everyone. To an always-hungry, growing girl, the round of cheese smelled every bit as good as roses with maybe an assist from the pickle barrel and the slabs of salt pork and sausage rings that ornamented the higher elevations.

The candy case! There was downright beauty with all the big glass jars tipped up on their flattened shoulders; the better to display such a mouth-watering variety. Even today the memory sets my salivary glands to working. Jawbreakers, licorice ropes, gumdrops, suckers, bonbons, and on and on until making a choice called for the ultimate in soul-searching.

A loaf of bread took but an instant whereas selecting my candy called for much one-footed perusal, bending as close to the case as glass panels permitted (the smudges I must have left!) until finally my mind was made up and Mr. Matthew's patience was rewarded.

"I'd like a penny's worth of that and that and that — mixed, please."

A friend rode down the street on her horse just as I was untying Topsy.

"Where you going?" I called happily. "Want some candy?"

"Over to see Johnny's new puppy. Wanta come?"

Having admired the young collie extravagantly, "He looks just like a Sunnybank pup," we went on to another friend's place and from there, who knows? With each stop the loaf of bread lost more and more of its new baked appeal; once it was forgotten and left behind but I retraced my steps soon enough to reclaim it. Finally some helpful soul provided me with a string to tie it to the saddle (chariot wheels?) until it was probably the most travelled loaf of bread thereabouts but I was true to my trust and never really lost it.

Riding home through the spring dusk that smelled of peonies and iris and just nameless green things and sweet, good earth I was at peace with the world. A fingernail moon in the western sky prompted sober thought until I found the proper wish.

There was another I should have made I learned when I sauntered into the kitchen and laid a pitiful loaf of bread on the table.

"Dorothy Lyons, just where have you been? Will you tell me — no, don't tell me," Mother cried with the anguish of one who has been blamed for "her child's" shortcomings for hours past. "Wherever it was go in and tell your father who has been waiting for you since this noon when there was no bread on the table."

Quick as a hummingbird's wing my wonderful day turned inside out to blackest fear. My father was not a patient man at best and the horror of my position flooded over me in waves of terror. Not fear of physical punishment; Dad was not a child beater, but he had his ways.

No condemned man's last mile was any harder than my heavy-footed progress from the kitchen into Dad's study. Silently I stood before him, my head bowed in shame, the story of my day written on my dirty clothes while all the joy of it had dissolved into air.

"What have you to say for yourself?"

"N-nothing — I j-just forgot. I'm sorry."

"Yes, I'm sure you are now, Dorothy, and just so that you *may*," his dwelling on this word was lost on me then, "remember the next time, you will not leave this place for one week."

This touched a nerve. "But it's spring vacation," I choked. "We're going to go —"

" 'They,' Dorothy, not 'we,'" he corrected steadily. "This will give you plenty of time to remember that a responsibility is not to be taken lightly. Sometime in your life more than a loaf of bread may be involved." He waited a moment to see if I had anything else to say. When I did not he resumed his reading. I slunk off unhappily yet knowing in the back of my mind I was getting off easily. He could have taken my horse!

All that week I drifted around like a ghost without a house to haunt, watching my happy friends' comings and goings, hearing their laughter and hoofbeats as they rode past. I made no attempt to talk with them; my sequestered state made me feel as though I was behind glass, both inaudible and invisible.

There was much I could have done. My tack would have profited from some time spent on it. Topsy would have enjoyed a more thorough grooming. I could have completed some of my outside reading assignments. Instead I moped. Softy that she was, Mother tried to temper the wind for her shorn lamb but the world was my enemy and I'd have none of it. One thing I did do, however, was reflect on the error of my ways. After that week's trauma cut deep into my consciousness, I was left with, "Be sure to do what you're told when you're told!" Dad was right. I have remembered it a long time.

Nor was he entirely the heartless judge. He knew what he was doing when he said "a week." That left me free the following weekend to broadcast my courtmartial and make light of it as if it hadn't mattered.

In telling Kit and her mother I unwittingly turned the clock back two centuries. "I don't know why he got so upset. They had cake there all the time!"

XVII

The homemaking arts were never one of my strongest suits. No one ever let me forget the time Mother was away for a day or two, probably one as as the ship fell apart without its captain for more than twenty-four hours, and I was appointed to get the supper.

I did after a fashion, although I have a faint recollection of raw meat and burned potatoes. When the others complained I felt that my defense was ironclad.

"Well, there are flowers on the table, aren't there?"

On reaching the eighth grade girls were automatically enrolled in the Domestic Science class (boys had shop or something). Our training included both cooking and sewing. The only teacher while I was there was a pale, willowy blonde who, along with just about every other female in high school be she student or teacher, had a crush on brother Don. Alice was very subject to colds and every cold went into laryngitis (a serious weakness in Michigan's climate). Two or three times a year she would come to class and state in something less than a stage whisper, "Girls, I expect you to be very good today because I've lost my voice."

That was as good as a battlecry for us. During cooking the dough flew about with lethal accuracy despite her most impassioned whispers. During sewing no one was safe from premeditated — but unexpected — encounters with the needle.

These classes were in another building near the center

of town as no schoolroom had been available with suitable amenities. Had I been commissioning the domestic science rooms I would have pasted opaque paper over the windows, for I am certain the outside was more interesting than the inside.

The street behind our classroom had hitching posts and tie racks for country shoppers who came by horse and buggy or wagon. One day while daydreaming out of the window I was electrified to see a team of horses that had come untied, ambling along on its own. Somehow they had gotten away from the other rigs without any real catastrophe and were just on their way home. Whether it was one or ten miles they knew the way. I wish I could say they were "running away" but in truth they were jogging slowly down the un-busy street. No matter! There was something that really needed my attention far more than a flatfell seam or a strawberry mousse.

Zipping out the door, down the hall, through the outer door I burst into the street like a cyclone. Remembering all I'd read about just such a crisis, I ran up alongside, grabbed a rein and pulled back while cajoling them.

"Whoa, boys, whoa. Where're you going?"

Obedient as always these big, beautiful beasts slowed down and stopped with slightly puzzled expressions.

Who was this girl-child giving them orders like she owned them?

Then I didn't know what to do with them. Their owner had not materialized and I felt sure my presence was practically a command performance back in the class. Finally a doctor whose offices were near took over for me and again I was the decorous student.

Whether or not I ever gained any proficiency in the gentle arts is debatable, but I moved along with my class into appropriately more difficult assignments. At last the day came when we were going to make a dress, not just potholders or laundry bags.

Connie and I hied ourselves to Rolland's Dry Goods Store to pick out our material and charge it. Colors were always my thing so I chose a pretty design of pink and lilac and white nosegays on a soft blue-gray background. Eventually as the earth turns our frockes were finished and so too was the school year.

As a sort of "victory dinner" we were being taken to Summit Heights, a dine and dance night spot on Long Lake, by an old friend of Connie's family. Later I wondered whatever prompted him to issue such an invitation, but we didn't question it then!

"The whole place has just been redecorated," Connie reported, "and all painted and fixed up real fancy."

Our anticipation knew no restraints.

"D'ya think anyone will ask us to dance? And will we know how if he does?"

My wardrobe was not extensive so what more appropriate than a summer-flowered dress? I was triumphant to have a new one for the occasion — and my sewing job was not half bad I decided as I admired myself in the mirror.

At last we started, arrived and headed for the dining room dance floor. As usual my eagerness had me in the forefront, too, too far to be able to fade away inconspicuously.

I was ahead all right, ahead of my time, for my dress material was flowered chintz, the identical flowered chintz as the entire dining room — curtains, valances, chair cushions and backs, even napkins. I've heard of women whose whole day is runied by seeing an identical dress; picture a large, large area filled with lights and music and a happy, gaily dressed throng and me with my protective coloration barely visible just fading into the background like a quail in a grassy meadow.

XVIII

"He's coming in on the noon train. We'll offer to pick him up at the station and bring him to the house. And then — Oh, boy!" They chortled with devilish glee.

Brother Don was the speaker and soon-to-be brother-in-law Warren DeYoung was the object of his conversation, for the moment of Sister Patricia's nuptials was at hand. Ordinarily the high jinks begin *after* the ceremony but not in the fiendish minds of Don and his cronies, both former suitors for the lady's hand.

"And we'll get Rome to arrest us and throw us in the jug," Don gloated.

The flivver, the only equipage available, was decorated with flags and streamers, and witty signs such as "Honeymoon Special," "Eat, Drink and Be Merry For Tomorrow Ye Shall Be Married," "Paradise Special — All Aboard for New Orleans," as the honeymoon couple would head for the Mardi Gras in time for the opening ball, the Rex Ball to close it, and ten days at a Biloxi, Miss. resort.

Sweeping Skinny (nee Warren) off the platform they raced up and down the main drag with horns blaring, streamers streaming, and rowdy voices in accompaniment. (The flivver in itself was a real, old-fashioned sound machine.) Speed limits made no difference, noise abatement had never been heard of and the helpless, hapless groom-to-be felt himself in a different wild west world from the quiet, orderly milieu he had so recently left.

Would he ever see his beautiful bride again? A surreptitious peek at his watch showed it was already past time for the strains of Lohengrin's Wedding March as played by his sister Leona to have turned all heads toward the stairway.

On the second or third pass down the main drag an impressive figure stepped off the curb and held up his hand. Rome, short for Romeo, the town marshall, who had been alternately the boys' friend or adversary over the years, according to which script they were playing out, would have been imposing at any time even without the majesty of the law behind him.

"Halt! You're all under arrest for disturbing the peace, exceeding the speed limit, violating Statutes XXVII, XXX

IV as well as Subsection 10 of Code 7." (Had anyone asked for clarification of these misdemeanors they would have proved hollow phrases.)

The poor bridegroom was well nigh speechless. To be put in the cooler when his adored bride was expecting him! To appear (if ever) before the wedding guests as a jailbird! What would Mr. and Mrs. Lyons think?

"Officer, couldn't we t-t-t-talk this over?"

"No, no, you young bloods have tried my patience long enough — and this is just too much. In with you." He emphasized this with a simulated push on Don's brawny shoulder.

"M-m-maybe we could give you some money —" Skinny began.

"Trying to bribe an officer of the peace," Rome roared. "That'll be another count against you."

"N-no, I meant no harm, only some sort of down payment on our bail - fine- sentence," Skinny mumbled miserably.

"Just shut up and get in there. Wait, you there, you city slicker, you look a little like Natty Nick. You'd better come with me. This cell's for you."

After turning the lock on Don and his friends Rome pseudo-shoved Warren into a separate cell and banged the door viciously, but he forgot to snap the lock. (Turned out that Dad had heard the plotting and hatched a counter plot that included keeping the others in the pokey until the 4:18 train had left for Detroit and New Orleans.)

If Warren had been confused before by now he began to doubt his sanity. The others didn't seem to be one bit worried, in fact they appeared to be enjoying the whole affair. After a short period of milling around they decided the joke had gone far enough and it was time to get on with the wedding.

"Oh, Rome. Hey, Rome," they bellowed. "Come let us out."

Only the echoing jail replied.

"Rome. Come on. Get us out of here."

But Rome had gone home to lunch. Warren, remembering he had not heard the lock click on his cell tried the door, and nothing before in his life had given him the joy he felt on finding it unlocked.

"I'm out, fellows," he whispered. "I'll go and get help for you."

He disappeared up the dilapidated steps toward sunlight but they had little hope of help from that quarter when he realized it was all a hoax.

Meanwhile back at the house on the hill the wedding guests had been thrown into complete confusion and consternation by a late arrival's report of the arrests and incarceration. Before anything could be done, however, the breathless, disarrayed bridegroom came panting in (he would have been panting worse if he hadn't found the flivver and added car theft to his other crimes by expropriating it. After all it had his wedding clothes and toilet kit in it, and he was a sight.)

"They're all in jail," he babbled. "Someone of influence must contact the president of the town council, pay their fines, arrange bail - anything to get them released."

He was not so magnanimous when it dawned on him that it was all a put up job, then they could have lain there and rotted for all of him. He rushed off to clean up for his wedding ceremony, now almost an hour late.

And what of the bride? Was she in tears, hysterics, where were the smelling salts, etc? No, indeed. She hadn't lived her life with those same young bucks without learning composure. She and her attendants were having a good laugh in the upstairs room that looked down the street toward town in the best "Is he coming, Sister Anne?" tradition.

The bridegroom's appearance was improved, the wedding party sans best man was assembling, wedding guests resumed positions like actors in a play regrouping after a break when a great commotion was heard at the back door. Three sweaty, wild-eyed young men mudstained to their knees burst into the kitchen.

"Has Rome been here looking for us? Have you heard anything from him?"

Nothing but blank faces greeted this outburst. Don went on.

"He doublecrossed us, but that old jail wouldn't hold a teaparty. We broke the door down, but then we didn't dare come through town so we came crosslots through the swamp and river. Can you hold off a little while longer, Sis?"

"Sure! What're a few more minutes?" Nonie replied with great good humor.

Only an hour late Lohengrin finally greeted several of the pinkest, most cerubic faces ever to attend a wedding but it is just possible that Warren took exception to the minister's "Dearly Beloved."

There were other friends of the bride and groom there that day too, and they became an informal posse to keep the evildoers under constant surveillance during the remainder of the afternoon, through the wedding collation in the tastefully decorated dining room until the principals had changed into their traveling clothes and were driven to the 4:18 train by responsible parties.

X X X

This report is based on the account of the wedding written for the two local weeklies, The Independent and The Courier, by the bride's mother, Mary Louise Adams Lyons, who always wanted to be a writer. It was also reproduced and given to guests at the DeYoungs' golden wedding anniversary party.

XIX

Reared on the traditions of Ralph Henry Barbour, indoctrinated in all the high principles of the teams at West Point and Annapolis, nurtured on the precepts of teams from the cricketeers of England to the bloodthirsty sports of India and Africa, I was nevertheless completely frustrated by force of circumstance. My school had a football team, boys only, and that was it.

My imagination battened on heroic exploits: my terrific returns broke Bill Tilden's serve; I outrode Tommy Hitchcock on his best polo ponies; time and again I made spectacularly long runs, 80, 90, 98 yards for the winning touchdown in uncounted and unknown football "big" games (who cared if girls could not play?)

Not until my sophomore year in high school did my dreams show any possibility of materializing. A new school had been built, or at least an enlargement across the front of the old which was gutted and transformed into a gymnasium. We girls could have a basketball team!

Filled with "derring-do" I went out for the team coached by one and the same Alice of Domestic Science background. I was light on my feet and fast, so naturally I was played at forward. Would that I could report I was a "natural," that without having ever played it before I instinctively knew all the right things to do. Not so.

I let the guards pocket me in so that I was worse than useless — another girl in my place *might* have done something — instead of playing tag all over the court. When team selections were posted it was no surprise to me that I was not on the first team.

Due largely to the lack of players I did qualify as a substitute forward. Our first game was scheduled with a consolidated school that had been in existence for some time. It was located in the center of a farming community and just about all the students were hearty, cornfed monsters.

I could hardly stand it when selections were being made for our first "away" game. Oh! the sound of it, the romance of it. Largely, I believe, due to the fact that Alice still had a yen for brother Don, I was down to go, a lowly sub to be sure but who'd complain so long as I could get on that magic bus carrying both the girls' and boys' teams?

Arriving, we suited up in our snazzy black sateen bloomers and white middies and trotted out on the court where the impact of the opposing Amazons left me breathless. Suddenly substitute didn't seem all that bad. Maybe I wouldn't have to go up against any of those female behemoths.

From the first whistle it was nothing but a slaughter of innocents. They scored on us when they wanted to with such ease it would have been insulting if we hadn't been so numb. Up and up the score went through the tens, the twenties, thirties, forties, fifties. Happily they were falling victim to the glut of baskets they were scoring and the numbers weren't rising quite as rapidly as at first.

The first quarter passed; half-time gave us a chance to lick our wounds in private; third quarter wore itself out while they were still in the sixties. During the last quarter Alice became conscious enough to remember her obligation to give Don's little sister a piece of the action. Certainly she could do little harm with the score 65-0.

At her nod I sprang up and pulled off my sweater and trotted out onto the court. I felt like a composite of an early Christian martyr and the main character in one of my fantasies, probably the one who gave up her life for the TEAM, as I faced my guard.

Evidently I was a better actor than basketball player, for my opponent was so impressed with my truculent manner she committed a personal foul against me. A sharp whistle signalled her crime. Play stopped and I was positioned on the foul line, the basketball in my hand to shoot at the basket a mile high and blocks away.

This *was* something I knew a little about. I had a good eye and had spent some time practicing free throws. I would go down trying! Drawing a bead on the basket I drew my arms back and let 'er fly. So intent was I on the path to the basket I almost felt myself flying through the air with the ball.

True as an arrow the ball and I went, up and up, then curved downward in a pretty arc that slipped through the basket so smoothly it hardly disturbed the netting. The Toonerville supporters went wild. We'd scored! We wouldn't be skunked. Who cared if the final score was something like 68-2? We had drawn blood.

And in a minor way my dazzling dreams were realized. I did not win the game for Toonerville BUT I was our high scorer!

XX

The weekend stretched before us alluringly. Connie had the whole two days off from her farm-ly chores; the weather was superb as only October in Michigan can be; aromas of ripening fruit, drying grasses and crops, even some pumpkin pie Mother was making spiced the air; but the biggest plus of all was Brother Bob was away, for most of the day at least.

We did not have the benefit of dozens of patented games to entertain us. Either we played the old stand-bys, none at all, or we made up some. We had hit on a happy combination for the latter. I had carelessly picked up a long pole such as would have a rake at the end but that was no longer true. Boy power had separated head and handle so effectively only the pole survived, and I carried it around. It had been in rapid succession a mountain-climbing staff, an oversize baton, a plain old prod to badger anything that happened along.

Somewhere I saw a largish ring like heavy draperies hang on. The pole slipped through it neatly. Nothing is ever static and soon I was flipping it into the air off the end and then running around beneath it trying to stab it back on. When it could be done the pole had to be flipped downwards instantly or the heavy metal ring would crack into the knuckles.

"Here, Connie, you do it a while."

She did it very neatly, so neatly I felt I must improve my form or be bested. By then we were trying for altitude too, just catching the ring was not enough. During one of my best flings Eldridge Locke, one of Bob's friends drove in looking for him. His mission was forgotten when he saw our "game of skill" and he had to have a turn.

He learned the hard way about snapping it down but smarting knuckles were no deterrent. Before he felt that he had had a long enough turn Shorty Wright drove in looking for Bob. Any contest, skill or not, challenges a teen-ager's pride so he had a turn. Connie and I hastily made some ground rules regulating the number of tosses, length of turns, and the like. The fellows could throw it higher, of course, but we insisted that was of no account.

We played singles, doubles, "challenge" matches, every kind of variation we could think of until our arms were sore from the unaccustomed motions, our necks from staring up into the sky, spots in our eyes from looking into the brightness, but stop we would not. They were captivated by our game (ring spearing is not a new game but I never heard of its being airborne) while Connie and I had the added thrill of having Bob's friends playing with us and treating us as equals.

Eldridge (I wonder if he had a nickname, I don't remember any) had a nice tenor and during his turn began singing "Not much money, oh, but honey, ain't we got fun!" and we truly did.

But, of course, it was too good to last. After awhile Bob drove in the yard in the rackety old T and instantly all four of us resumed our accustomed roles: baby sister, friend of same, lordly high school friends of big brother. Maybe it's just as well though as we had wrung just about everything possible out of the game.

Many times memory has gone back to that happy afternoon whether because of our new "equality," the spontaneity of our homemade game, or possibly the stars in their courses were just right for that day. I know Connie remembered it; I wonder if Eldridge or Shorty ever did.

XXI

Like heat lightning flickering along the horizon there was talk of moving away from Toonerville but I paid no more notice than I would have of real heat lightning. Not anyway until the thunderbolt struck! We were going to move. As soon as the house was sold.

Mother tried to soften the blow for me somewhat but there was just no way it could be done. Away was away and nothing could change it.

"But why?" I asked miserably. "We're all happy here. We've got a beautiful place. Why go somewhere else?" I barely suppressed a choke.

"You can see just as well as we can, Dorothy. With three of you children in college at the same time, two right now the only way we can manage it is to live where you won't have to pay board and room.

"Besides, it will be much better for your father's work. Being in the textbook business a college town is a natural for his headquarters: he'll be able to see and talk with educators and others prominent in the field; also he'll be able to be at home more since time he spends there will now be home time and not travel time."

"But — but — but," was the best I could come up with.

"You'll like it there once you get used to it. Lots more young people and things to do. Just try to think of it that way and you'll soon change your mind."

"Never."

As usual I raced for the barn to share my troubles with Topsy. This time it only compounded my woe! Topsy! I never could take her to Ann Arbor. And just when I'd gotten such a dandy outfit together: a sporty, rubbery-tired buggy and a pretty good harness with lots of patent leather after all the beat up ones I'd used; a cutter with *doors* and springs even! My dog! What would happen to her?

At this crowning blow I dissolved in such misery even

Topsy was moved to touch my head with her nose, an unusual gesture of concern. I finally pulled myself together on the hope the house wouldn't sell — ever! — and life could go on as it was, not stopping to think of winter-time when Mother and I were the only ones home five days out of the week, carrying coal from the basement up one or two flights for three greedy, top-loading coal stoves.

That straw soon blew away in the winds of change as some local people jumped at the chance to buy "the Lyons' house on the hill." Mother and Dad began their househunting in Ann Arbor in earnest and almost before I could hope they wouldn't find anything they liked they were home with word they had put money down on a nice brick house between town and campus, reasonably priced with terms that could be tailored to those they were giving on the Toonerville place.

From there it was all downhill on a slide that accelerated to a frenzied pace. Topsy presented no problem as she could be taken out to our farm, but where or who got my other prized possessions I can't recall out of the blur of misery that took hold of me. My wonderful old saddle that a neighbor's grandfather had ridden all through the Civil War was to go with me and hang in the basement — "if I ever have the money I'm going to have one made just like that," I vowed. I knew a good thing when I saw one and that saddle was the most comfortable one I ever rode. Later I realized it was the forerunner of the McClellan saddle so hated by all cavalry recruits but somehow the comfort had been lost in its "improvement."

I went around saying "good-bye" to all my friends and acquaintances, for though I'd be back often and they would come to visit me we knew it was the end of an era. Only the English language has no other word softer than good-bye. There's "auf wiedersehn," "a riverderci" "au revoir" "sayonara" and "hasta luego" but only English has the uncompromising, irrevocable thud of "good-bye" and only that.

The final thrust was delivered by the immense van on moving day: for years Mother had a cherished plant she had sent away for; if the baseball rolled into it we held our breaths; no hoof should fall on it, when to my horror I saw the big, dual wheels of the van crunch right across it. The end. Good-bye.

XXII

It was once said that Britain's battles were won on the playing fields of Eton. From my limited experience I'll believe it. Certainly, some of my most important lessons were learned through playing games.

Before I could try out for another basketball team in Toonerville, the Lyons clan pulled up stakes and roots and heartstrings and moved to Ann Arbor. There as a new girl in a strange school I kept a pretty low profile, not that there were any teams to try for.

Two years later when I entered the University I was overjoyed to find a full athletic program for girls, field hockey in the fall, basketball during the winter and who could play anything but baseball during the spring! In high school I had held a hockey stick in my hands once or twice during a very disjointed gym period, so when a friend said she was going out for the freshman field hockey team and why didn't I come along it seemed sheer madness.

She coaxed me as she didn't want to go alone and I agreed. At first that too seemed pretty disjointed but as time wore on a pattern could be sorted out.

The coach had two teams, presumably first and second, for which she kept drawing on girls along the sidelines. Meanwhile the rest of us played around, I seeing how hard and far I could hit the ball.

Later the coach came over and said, "Which of you girls thinks you can hit the ball pretty hard?" This was no time for modesty, so I had no hesitation in allowing it would take a hefty girl to do it better.

"All right, go in there at right fullback."

On such chances are reputations made. Always before I had been put in at forward like in basketball because I was fast and quick, but here at last was my niche.

I completely lacked any aggressive desire to cross the opponent's goal line, but just let them challenge mine and I was a tiger! Not only that but being fleet of foot I could "run with the hare and hunt with the hounds" — play up almost with the forward line but if any opposing player got past me I could overhaul her and be between her and our goal line in a twinkling. Also, I could reach out a stick at a ball bounding by and almost like magic catch and deflect it, how even I never knew.

That was a storybook season. I made the first team and saved many a goal.

Even in a defensive position, basketball was not my bag, but come spring and baseball I was johnny-on-the-spot. What position to go for I had no idea as all my other baseball games had been one-ol'-cat where one worked up from field with every out until after a turn at bat one went back to field again. I knew where the best games were in Toonerville and would ride Topsy there, tie up and play for a few turns, then mount and go on to another game until oncoming darkness foreshadowed a reluctant end to the day.

"Try third base, Dorothy," the coach said (one and the same coach as for hockey).

That was all right and I made the team, probably because if I threw a ball at a target I usually hit it. Our very first game was with the preceding year's champions. They weren't champions for nothing, and before we knew it the bases were loaded and one of their best hitters coming up.

The runner on third base, mine, was a frisky one who kept threatening to steal home, but not if our pitcher could stop it. I have always thought she must have been drafted from the major leagues for she could sock that old ball until coming at me it looked like a rocket. Grimly I'd put my hands up in front of my face, more to protect myself, I think, than to keep that runner on base. By some miracle I neither dropped it nor let her "accidentally" jar it out of my hands.

She died on third (as I almost did too). I've no recollection of how the game turned out but holding that runner on third through an entire inning was a tour de force not lost on other teams and players. Be it known, however, that after that game I shifted to short stop where I played happily for my whole four years.

I could hardly contain myself until fall and hockey season rolled around. I was a tiger, wasn't I? I'd burn up those fields. Like a dash of cold water I found that the coach had forgotten me, gone was the glory of my miraculous saves, my tremendous wallops, and I spent most of my time on the sidelines with the hopefuls.

This was pretty hard to take for a while. "I'll just quit and not go back. No use!" Then Don's words echoed through my head. "Somebody's got to play on the second team so's the first team gets practice."

With those words I cooled down and kept at it, giving the first team something to really practice on with my long drives and fancy footwork. Finally when team selections were made, there I was at my darling position, right fullback.

"She knew all the time what I could do and was just finding out about the others," I told myself happily as I raced around the field filled with the elation of success.

And success it was. Not only did I have a banner season but when the hockey banquet signalled end of season I made the All-Star Team. We all wore colored jerkins of our class team colors and, as names were called, the player went up in front to stand with others picked for the honor. Few times in my life have I ever been so thrilled. From the season's start when I felt less than nothing to stellar status was heady stuff.

At the time Michigan women's teams did not play

intercollegiate games but in my own mind this honor was equivalent to making the varsity my sophomore, junior and senior years.

There in hockey and baseball I learned two or three lessons that have stayed with me all my life: don't try to go against your nature; do the very best you can even when it looks hopeless; keep trying whether or not you think you are appreciated — it may turn out all right.

So much for the playing fields of Eton.

XXIII

The local paper's astrologer is always commenting on how much Sagittarians like to travel, so I come by my itchy feet honestly. After graduation I stayed at home for another year whilst learning the black arts of shorthand and typing, always with a view to packing up and hurrying off somewhere else to gain my fame and fortune.

Despite having been born and brought up in what scientists laughingly call the temperate zone I loathe cold weather with a holy passion. Therefore, my fame and fortune should await me in a warm climate and California became Mecca. Parents being parents, however, Mother and Dad were set against my going west because of a hot affair I was having (by mail) with a young fellow in Seattle which, to midwesterners, was just around the corner from California.

Family councils, even the sketchiest discussions, always ended in a tempestuous free-for-all. Many times I have wondered how different my life might have been had I come to California — and Hollywood — in those early days. Not that I had professional stage ambitions, though I love to ham it up in front of footlights, but my writing bent might well have landed me in some interesting if not lucrative jobs. Oh, well! "Of all sad words of tongue or pen —"

Finally in the interests of family harmony Nonie arbitrated the deadlock.

"Why," she asked, "don't you go to New York instead for a few years? A spell in NYC never hurt anyone's image and might be lots of fun."

We drew back to think things over and it didn't seem like a bad idea at all. So the die was cast. I had been working in one of the University departments as a green, very green, stenographer, saving up my money for a trip.

It really was kind of dirty because being the youngest the folks had me pegged for the little helpmate who would stay at home, fetch things, help around, light pipes, etc. and to be living on their largess while saving my money to take wing was hardly playing it fair. But who said children are fair!

The Depression was rapidly becoming more of a canyon but I gaily made my plans, while pinching pennies until the Indian screamed for mercy. At last I accumulated a grubstake. When I gave notice at my temporary job and told them my plans my kindly old employer said gently, "Miss Lyons, I admire your spirit but not your judgment. We'll miss you and be glad to welcome you back."

My three college summers I had waited on tables at Lake Placid Club in the Adirondacks (such happy times) and several of my eastern friends had gravitated to New York City. Also, and this loomed large in my plans, a Club guest had said if I ever decided to come to New York there'd be a place in his company for me.

Letters went out hither and yon. Arrangements were made to room with two friends and a stranger up near Columbia in a big flat rented by an enterprising woman and sublet to people like us. Everything wasn't all bright though as my intended benefactor replied his company had moved to outer New Jersey/Mongolia but I was still welcome. Welcome-smelcome! He could have it except in direst straits.

My luck was strong, as always, and I had a job within ten days of my arrival even with soup kitchen lines three blocks long. To be sure, the company went bankrupt six months later but by then I had my connections.

"If you ever hear of a steno job, better let me know," I said to one. "Mine is going to fold momentarily."

And later that very week his boss said to line up some secretary prospects as she was letting hers go. An appointment was made for my lunch hour and I buzzed up on the subway, allowing plenty of time to spare in case of delays. And at the risk of repeating myself, there is just no substitute for that stupid Irish luck. Or is it hunch?

I was walking down the hall toward the door where I could see the words "National Association of Book Publishers" though I knew I was early. There was an open window and just on a whim I stopped and leaned out, admiring the New York scene until the clocks were striking twelve, when I walked into the office.

Many times later when anyone showed up early for an appointment my boss fussed and fumed as though it was a federal offense.

I have always been one for long range, very long range, planning which used to confound Mother every once in a while. Like in December I would say, "Mama, can I go to the Sunday School picnic next June?" How could you answer that? So she'd parry with "We'll cross that bridge when we get to it," thereby throwing me into complete frustration.

Several years later Connie and I were looking into a store window that was packed with little framed, illustrated mottos when I saw just the one. The next time she pulled that bridge-crossing routine I drew up in a dignified fashion and said, "Yes, many people believe that but I prefer what Bruce Barton said, 'I do not like the phrase, "Cross a bridge when you get to it." The world is owned by men who crossed bridges in their minds miles ahead of the procession.' " So that was that.

(One digression I cannot resist, another motto in the window on, I believe, a pillow cover with a picture of conifers, "I pine for you. Spruce up and come, for when I'm lonely I balsam.")

Anyway during my last years in New York I was yearning for blue skies and a hot sun, so began laying more plans. They came to a head one day in January when Connie wheeled up to my New York apartment in Prairie Moon. We loaded all my chattels, what I had not given away or loaned, and left for Michigan the next morning. That was some trip during one of Ol' Man River's rampages with first one route, then another closed! Sufficeth to say we did make it.

Getting from Michigan to California presented fiscal problems. Years ago, before large motor transports, there were what were called drive-aways in which cars were driven long distances either in caravan or separately. Through his auto connections in Detroit Don arranged for me to drive a new Plymouth through to the coast.

One of my Ann Arbor friends agreed to ride with me and finally after I spent a week or two at home we left on the first leg, to Evanston to stay overnight with Nonie. She had a big party for us, so we were dragging a little as we left the next morning.

I hadn't wanted to be burdened with winter clothes in Hawaii and had decided to wear my spring topcoat and suit west. Our first day was balmy and delightful. The day we left Evanston the mercury had plummeted into the basement and in those days it was felt that a California car needed no heater.

Every time I thought I was going to freeze to death I'd stop and buy another newspaper to wrap around me. By evening we seemed to be swimming through a carful of papers that came up to the glass level in the doors without helping much.

Have I said before there is no substi----- I have? Oh. Even the famous-infamous west coast maritime strike of 1937 was not proof against my Irish luck, being settled whilst we were driving across the plains. Need I say that Matson Lines offices in San Francisco were just one notch less than a riot? Happily, this rioter was able to get a berth on the first ship bound for Hawaii after the strike although an Australia-run ship had touched there.

Two of my Adams cousins already lived in Honolulu; to them I had written of my ambitions. Joe was Attorney General of the Islands; his sister Florence was a teacher at Punahou Academy, the historic school to which early Californians sent their children by clipper ship rather than risk the perils of a trip overland or by sea across Panama or around the Horn.

Florence replied in a very discouraging vein, telling how many mainland girls came looking unsuccessfully for work but that it was plentiful in San Francisco or Los Angeles. Why didn't I go there instead?

"I'll get it on the way back then if it's so easy, but I'm sure going to give Honolulu a try," I resolved. My preparations had been careful and thorough, so on reaching my Promised Land I had only to go from the boat to pre-arranged accommodations. I did not get in touch with the cousins, however, until after I had a job, demonstrating a determination Dad had learned about years earlier.

Meanwhile Joe had read my name in the ship's passenger list and called every hotel on the island without locating me. Fernhurst, the YWCA residence, had not occurred to them. I had made my point. Several shipboard acquaintances wanted me to do this or that and go here or there with them but I kept saying, "Wait until I get a job and know how much money I can spend."

A few days after landing I attended the opening of the Hawaiian Legislature (not your usual opener with legislators doing the hula and singing Island songs). While waiting for things to get under way I bought a Star-Bulletin which carried an ad for a stenographer, needed immediately, can hand application in at classified ad desk of Star-Bulletin, etc. I rushed home, typed up the letter of application my NYC roommate and I had devised which was 100% as it had never failed to get a reply, whether or not we might want the job.

Days went by without a reply making me feel I should not tear around like a tourist. Reluctantly I decided that at last the letter had failed. A week later I had a phone call from the Star-Bulletin itself asking me to come down the next day for an interview. I busied around getting my clothes ready, my white shoes whitened and everything all set which was a very good thing.

That night shipboard friends took me driving and we wound up at Lau Yee Chi's handsome restaurant in the beach area. When they wanted me to have a drink I refused.

"Goodness, no. I've got to have a clear head for tomorrow."

"Well, a glass of wine won't hurt you."

Had I known then what I know now! I am allergic to wine and on two small glasses I had the worst hangover in history — slept through my alarm, woke just in time to throw my clothes on, no shower, no breakfast (and me with low blood sugar and a hangover). I raced out and luckily caught an open-air streetcar. I sank back and relaxed a moment. Too much! The wind blew my new hat off (fancy handwoven lauhala, $5.). I grabbed the cord and stopped the car, babbling to the motorman about my new hat, raced back to pick it up, only to see the car and its low-lived, no-good, insensitive oaf of a motorman disappearing down King street.

There wasn't another car in sight. Time was too short to wait, so I started chugging down the sidewalk toward the Star-Bulletin blocks away. Just try that on an outsize head filled with an ache that bounced back and forth from one temple to another beneath a tropical sun making your eyeballs about to fall out on the sidewalk in front of you.

Arriving I gasped my name and message to the girl on the desk and sank back in the chair gratefully.

"Mr. Allen will see you now."

Then and there I gave up any idea of ever getting the job but I had to go through with the whole agonizing sequence. Mr. Allen was a very pleasant, pink-cheeked man whose interview was not very formidable. Until . . .

"I'd like to give you a shorthand test — if you don't

mind, of course."

He bent over, rustled around in his lower drawer and withdrew the most fiendish torture instrument known to the business world. For those of you who don't know, Gregg shorthand is based on the English language, word beginnings, word endings, sound combinations. Much of his test material is graven on my brain forever. It began..

"Among the atolls and archipelagos of Melanesia, Micronesia and Polynesia" and went on about the Japanese mandated islands, the Versailles treaty, Der Fueher, Mein Kampf, and only the Inquisition knows what else. Once I bit off a burst of wild laughter and kept on keeping on.

He turned me over to his secretary who sat me down at an empty typewriter. Wouldn't you think Fate was through toying with me? No! Either the floor wasn't level or the chair casters were imperfect, for the chair rocked gently from side to side until I tried to correct it, then it went fore and aft.

"Don't panic, Dorothy. Cool head main thing. Just do it one word at a time."

Which I did only to have my demoralization complete when I saw the secretary glance at her watch and jot down the time I finished. Then I knew it was hopeless.

Nevertheless I kept putting off my friends and their big plans until I had work. At long last a week later I had another call from the Star-Bulletin. "Could I come down again for a few minutes?" Sure, sure. I went down and had a short interview by Senator Farrington, Publisher, after which Mr. Allen said, "You can just hang your hat over there and this will be your desk."

"Now?" I said dejectedly as if I hadn't just gotten a job in jobless Hawaii.

I still haven't seen the Island of Kauai. Had intended going there for my summer of '42 vacation.

Hawaii and I were made for each other. I was going to live the rest of my life there and, returning to the mainland in 1941, I packed up all my dearest treasures and took back with me. I began reading real estate ads but very little Hawaii property is in "fee simple," much more being in leasehold, and it went against all my deepest Irish feeling. After all, we had only owned our own land for two generations.

The Honolulu Star-Bulletin held me until one of my scouts told me of this great job with the Red Cross in the Dillingham Building. I applied for it and Mr. Gray, Chapter secretary, told me it was mine except for the fact that Mr. Allen, my present boss, was Chairman of the Chapter. When I told him I wanted to leave, account of good pay, etc. he looked at me a moment and asked, "What would you need to stay?" A real problem! If I put it too high he'd think I was an egotistical fool, if too low he'd meet it — and I wanted to go. Finally I dredged up, "I'm afraid I've gone too far to back track."

So I began my employment by the American Red Cross in Hawaii which continued through a short stint with the Los Angeles Chapter and several years as Executive Secretary of the Santa Barbara Red Cross.

My first book was begun while living in New York and so homesick for the outdoor life I had known. I reeled off nine pages the first year, sixteen the second but as a mark of my determination I did half of it before leaving for Hawaii and completed it a few months after arriving. Then I found how very, very far it is from Honolulu to New York City, the publishing center.

The third publisher I submitted it to accepted it. The first I had hoped would not take it, sending it there fulfilled an unwary promise. The second was very complimary but rejected it as "not quite ringing the bell." Sufficient time had passed for me to see at once why it had not.

Now, should any of you have writing ambitions, I proffer my Capsule Course in Fiction Writing. First get a plot, a good one with problems and conflict — not just straight narrative. Then flesh it out with characters, either good, believable people or bad, believable people or both. Put them in suitable surroundings where they are at home and which are plot/suitable. Conversation, of course, everywhere. Whenever possible add to realism by drafting the five senses: even in moments of highest drama "she heard a distant dog barking" or "the smell of new leather would always carry him back . . ." etc. Mix thoroughly, letting the characters live their own lives without any real or evident manipulation from you, carrying them toward a seemingly inevitable conclusion.

BUT then you inject an "all is lost!" The main character's hopes of ever achieving his/her most cherished objective are dashed to pieces and there can be no hope of winning through *until* by his/her own efforts or cleverness the catastrophe is reversed, the good guys come out on top and the bad guys get their comeuppance.

My book did not have an "all is lost," but remember, you read it here first. I knew my New York contact would have sent it on to Harcourt, Brace by then.

"When it comes back I'll have her hold it." It didn't come back although the children's editor felt it needed "something." My idea was just right, she thought, and I went on from there.

Over the following thirty odd years I wrote eleven more — all horse stories for teen-agers: girl wants horse, girl gets horse, girl loses horse or other important consideration, all turns out well. Many of these books I wrote during full-time employment; my second cost me twenty pounds.

At least I blame it on the book although my schedule was a killer. The Red Cross had launched its first war fund drive but Hawaii was low man on the totem pole and we were always a step or two behind in personnel additions. Many days I worked ten, eleven, twelve hours a day. I had just bought my colt Sunny who *had* to be exercised — I'd allow myself fifteen minutes lie-down after dinner and then to the typewriter. Some nights I'd find myself swaying with exhaustion but I'd said I was working on a book when I wasn't. Then they set a deadline. Did I work then!

A year later I returned to the mainland for good and for a time lived with my sister and her family in the San Fernando Valley. That was during my work as District Secretary with the Los Angeles Chapter of the Red Cross. Mother and Dad had come to the coast because of Mother's pneumonia susceptibility and we were all together. Such a happy time for all of us.

California and horses go together like apple pie and cheese and very shortly I was a horse owner again. It was not until my long love affair began with the Connemara pony, however, that my horse-related activities became so satisfying. The Irish Connemara is a large pony — in Ireland it's a pony but over here in the land of milk and honey some of them don't know when to stop growing.

A product of its environment, the Connemara evolved over many centuries, the harsh climate weeding out the weaklings, the rocky terrain requiring the best hoofs and legs for survival. In a primitive culture women tilled the soil so the lazy, the tricky were weeded out, to produce what the Connemara is today: a hardy, versatile, sweet-tempered animal so people-oriented it is happiest when working with man, especially if this be jumping.

I brought the first ones to California in 1963 where I have raised them, shown them, ridden them, loved them. Too, I served the American Connemara Pony Society in several capacities including two years as president. These Connes' are real hams so parades are a natural. On my macho, talented, versatile Kilkerrin Paddy (he was herd sire for fourteen years) I have ridden in many Santa Barbara Fiesta Parades as well as strutting our stuff in the Rose Parades of 80, 81 and 82. That was me on the handsomest horse in the parade!

Trail riding is a favorite horseback activity in California. Years ago, (thirty, I believe) several of us rode into the back country to camp for a few days. This was the beginning of the Santa Barbara Sage Hens, an exclusively women's group that rides out one week and two weekends each year. Now I'm the only active charter member.

Makes me feel something like the Great Stone Face.

As the war years' gung-ho spirit faded, trying to whip up any public spirit among Red Cross volunteers grew harder and harder. Mine too, and so I "retired" to the life of a writer. Alas! I'd rather play than work. After twelve years the inevitable happened: the shrinking dollar, expanding prices, TV competition, children's inability to read made it imperative that I become a wage slave again.

I found a spot as a secretary in the California Department of Industrial Relations and there I spent the remainder of my "productive" years. It was a pleasant job, eight to five, no troubles to carry home, no phone calls at all hours. One malicious co-worker was my only cross to bear. I always liked secretarial work, typing voluminous documents is a challenge, nor was the position so demanding but what I could juggle some of my personal projects simultaneously. Nevertheless, I felt I always gave good measure, fulfilling whatever commitment there may have been, contrary to some peoples' picture of the public servant.

Because of my late entry into the pension picture I had to work a year beyond Social Security's magic 62. But retirement! Oh, bliss. Oh, joy! The only thing that makes getting old worthwhile.

To help out with expenses I began selling horse food supplement as well as marketing Tackare, a saddle soap kit for saddlery care. For a while my income tax returns embraced about as many schedules as the IRS uses.

At the urging of two friends who incorporated with me, I wrote and they conducted a direct mail business known as the Dorothy Lyons Horsemanship School to sell the Dorothy Lyons Basic Horsemanship Course. I just can't figure out why it didn't go over bigger. It is a good course and those who enrolled were well satisfied (except one sorehead who got her money back). Someday (that's my kiss of death for any project) I'd like to turn it into a paperback do-it-yourselfer.

About the time I retired I was having trouble with my back, had gone off too many horses. Just in case I'd have to give up riding I began taking art lessons through the Adult Education program. Now I'm hooked - I found a good osteopath who fixed my back, so I have to find time for another time-consumer. I'll never rival Rembrandt or even the least in an artists' encylopedia, but it certainly is deeply satisfying.

My pictures are representational, I guess you'd say, not any one favorite subject. I just paint whatever turns me on. Some fellow artists think they're good. At least they're good enough to have won four awards as well as acceptance into both the Santa Barbara Art Association and Goleta Valley Art Association.

Writing is certainly my first love but painting is lots more fun. No need to shut the door, turn off the phone and hang up "No Admittance" signs. Several people can paint in the same room. For a while you paint like crazy, then everyone pauses, walks around and looks at the others' canvases, discusses problems or satisfactions, then back at it again.

XXIV

Sunday morning our riding group was having a breakfast ride to Waialae. I was looking forward to it because I would be sporting new English boots in a rich brown. Saturday night I set my alarm to allow plenty of time.

It dragged me from some far place I was reluctant to leave, so I turned over for a few more winks, figuring I could cut corners and still be on time. I had hardly closed my eyes again when planes began swooping and snarling overhead and distant guns added to the reality of the occasion.

"Well, if they're going to hold maneuvers on Sunday morning I might just as well get up." I fumed, slipping quickly into my riding clothes.

Down in the residential hotel's dining room I ordered breakfast and picked up the Honlulu Advertiser. Before I'd seen the first article, Verna, the girl who shared my stair landing, came rushing in in her housecoat, her hair uncombed, her usually placid face distorted with fright.

"Oh, Dorothy, the radio says the Japanese are attacking Pearl Harbor!"

"Verna sweetie, you know they've been having maneuvers for days now. Go on back to bed and get your rest."

"I don't know, Dorothy. It sounds awfully real."

The other few early risers in the dining room had heard her and came over to my table, among them a friend's son.

"Bobby, here's my key. Run up and get my portable radio, will you?"

He was back in a moment and the radio set up on my table.

"Don't be alarmed, folks. The situation is under control."

"There you see, Verna. I told you there was nothing to worry about."

She mumbled something about not being sure. Then the radio crackled again.

"Attach hoses to the faucets on your houses. Put buckets of sand up on the roof. Get your cars off the street even if you have to pull up over the curb."

"My, they're making it real, aren't they? But why aren't we having music in between the announcements" I fretted. "We always have music."

Another period of silence before Webb Edwards, my favorite announcer, came back on and spoke the time-honored words that made believers of us all.

"This is not a maneuver, folks. This is the real McCoy!"

Just then Verna's waitress, a soft-eyed Japanese girl in kimona and obi, brought her her customary breakfast.

"Oh, I can't eat now. It's all so terrible," Verna quavered.

"You sit down there and eat your breakfast" I commanded like a top sargeant. "You don't know when you'll eat next."

Despite Webb's veto of street travel several of us decided to go down to the beach, a block away, where by the curve of the bay we could look across to Pearl Harbor. Standing right at the sidewalk's edge we'd all start and run pellmell across the street, down through backyards and out into Kalakaua Avenue.

The black smoke of burning oil tanks billowed upward like a volcano. We were too far away to see any air activity or naval casualties. We stood there debating our next move when mine came to me in a flash. I was assistant secretary at the Red Cross! I'd better get back to my telephone.

Leaving the others I returned on the double and was just going up my stairs when the phone rang.

"Pick up whoever you can and get to the office right away." The boss, a soft-spoken southern gentleman, wasted no words. "You handled the dispersal of all our emergency medical supplies and we'll surely need them. Especially tannic acid. The burn cases are desperate."

Stopping only to pick up what was left of my birthday box of candy and a half-empty bottle of whiskey I went down to my little car and drove off into a different world.

I reported to the Red Cross office where I tried to be many places: first of all, sifting throught the countless manifests of thousands of dollars worth of medical supplies shipped to us only months before. While poring over the long yellow sheets I recalled the Board meeting when a local doctor expressed his concern.

"In the event of a major disaster we would not have a tenth of the supplies we would need — and the mainland is four and a half days away. I think we would be remiss not to have a large - very large - stock of medicines and equipment on hand.'

"That will cost thousands - hundreds of thousands, Joe. Who's to pay?" another asked.

"We wouldn't question it if we were in the middle of a disaster. Let's just order them and worry about paying later."

From the supplies I rushed over to the production department where ladies for months had been knitting garments, rolling bandages, making guaze squares. After that I don't know where all I went, only that sunset found me at an evacuation center at the University. Supper was beans and lettuce, and lucky we felt to have had a hot meal.

Every place I had been that day I met an airman with a stony face and a glazed look in his eyes as he asked for information on his wife and son.

"I left them in the Hickam Housing just minutes before THEY came in. Went back as soon as I could - no one there - house pocked by machinegun bullets. Oh, God, if I could only find them safe."

Since I would be driving back downtown I offered the desolate man a ride to help him on his search. While waiting for him I stood outdoors in the gathering gloom and looked at the flag proudly showing all its stars and stripes at the administration building's pole.

It was already blackout, meaning that all cars' lights were painted black except for a two-inch circle in the center which was dark blue, not really very helpful.

Our staff had been divided in two. Half, including me, would spend the night at the main office; the other half come to work the next morning. As if Nature was complying with the Military Governor's orders a cloud cover came up to blot out even the starshine. From our third floor windows we peered down into velvety blackness so complete it hurt the eyes. Once in a while we could hear tramping feet. Several times fusillades of shots ripped the night.

"Boy, there isn't money enough in the world to pay me to go down there," a field director said. And I agreed.

The phone rang, for the millionth time. This time it was one of our people farther out at Production Center.

"Here comes a big flight of planes."

Before the words were said the planes were over us. We could only stare through the dark at the whites of each other's eyes, not knowing whether they were friend or foe — and we were just across the street from the Hawaiian Electric power plant and one block from the harbor. An instant later they were over Hickam Field which lit up with antiaircraft fire, tracer bullets, a burning building.

Silhouetted against this illumination I could make out the American flag still flying on the American Factors Building. For how long? I wondered silently.

We had little time to worry for the phones were never open, one call coming on top of another so rapidly there was no time for it even to ring. All the fears and terrors that crowded in during this tension-filled, uncertain night demanded reassurance. And where to get it but from the Red Cross? Some were legitimate, others so outlandish they helped relieve our own tensions with some good laughs.

Sometime in the middle of the night things quieted down enough to realize our bodies were screaming for rest. I went into the wool room where it was doled out to knitters and tried without any luck to arrange the shanks from a cartonful on a table. That shiny table top kept crowding up through them.

Slowly, grudgingly a dank, gray dawn arrived. As soon as it was light enough to relax the curfew I sent the staff home since the phones had not started up yet.

"I can hold the fort until the others come," I assured them, thinking longingly of a shower and bed.

To stay awake I turned on the little office radio. The first thing I heard was . . . . "the President of the United States of America." From that President Roosevelt launched into his "date that will live in infamy" speech culminating in asking Congress to declare that a state of war had existed between Japan and the United States since the morning of December eighth. At the conclusion of his speech the band played The Star-Spangled Banner.

I was so moved I turned to look out at the harbor, the sky, the mountains, my country with its flag bravely flying above Aloha Tower.

"Oh, say can you see by the dawn's early light." *This* dawn.

"What so proudly we hailed at the twilight's last gleaming" — Sunset and blackout at the University.

"Whose broad stripes and bright stars through the perilous night o'er the ramparts we watched were so gallantly streaming" — The Amfac building could have been fortifications.

"And the rocket's red glare, the bombs bursting in air gave proof through the night that our flag was still there" — Planes, bombs, tracers, fire over Hickam.

"Oh, say does that star-spangled banner yet wave o'er the land of the free and the home of the brave?" My eyes were spilling over as I visualized mountains, prairies, meadows, cities.

Now when the national anthem is played I want to sing along with it, but I never can. My heart is so full it rises up in my eyes - my throat - and chokes me, making song-speech - impossible.

XXV

The thick, brown hair braid coiled across my desktop like the snake in Eden. Tentatively I picked up the end and dipped it in my inkwell.

"You do that again and I'll give you a good pinch."

So, of course, I did it again. And the avenging angel gave me such a monumental pinch I can recall the pain to this day.

On such events was my friendship with the slight, brown-haired, brown-eyed fifthgrader forged so durably that now, sixty-seven years later, we are still "veribest friends."

Connie lived with her folks on a farm four miles north of town which was the only thing that prevented our being together 24-hours a day. We both had horses and a love of the outdoors that would keep us probing the byways for years.

A few weeks after we first met I was invited to come out to the farm Friday after school for a visit. I was all ready to don my pants (whatever they were, it was years before jeans), and boots but Mother was aghast.

"Dorothy Lyons, you are not going visiting for the first time looking like a ragamuffin. You will wear your white dress and look like a well-brought up young lady."

Brother Bob was delegated to take me out in the flivver and pick me up later in time to be home by bedtime. When I stepped down out of the Ford in my grandeur — not only was it white, it was lace with a hundred little bobbing petals (I must have been a vision) Connie's face said it all.

I looked down shamefacedly without meeting her eye. "Mother made me wear it," I explained without preamble.

Not one to let trifles slow us down, however, we covered her lakefront, the woods, the barn from the stables to the hay loft, the calf pen, the puppy run. Understandably, I never wore that dress again. It was October and the late afternoon grew chill, even cold which wetted my appetite that never needed any stimulus.

Her mother's voice calling us to supper was worthy of the Met. There was a big pan of "fried potatoes," now called hashed brown, on the stove, and their aroma would have made me more than willing to sell my birthright. Without any preamble I hurried to the stove, held my eager nose just above the pan and breathed soulfully.

"My, but that smells good."

On many occasions over thirty years I walked into their kitchen and Mrs. Conrad always greeted me with, "Hungry, Dorothy?" And I always was!

For six years we chummed together as much as our distant homes permitted, but then the worst happened. My family moved to Ann Arbor.

This distance was a real obstacle to our many plans and expeditions. Long distance was only for emergencies so the U.S. Mail got our business. Not until then did we discover how really close we were, for whenever we were trying to work out details of some big plan as sure as one of us wrote a letter, the other did too and they always crossed in the mail. Finally we began planning for this and would say something like if you write thus-and-so, we'll do this but if you say such and such, we'll do that.

This went on for four years while we finished high school and Connie put in two years of junior college before she too came to Ann Arbor and roomed with me. Once out of college she got a job in Detroit and I lit out for those "far away places." Connie married and had two girls but we kept in close contact as well as we could but the intervals between letters grew longer and longer, tho the tie was still there.

One morning driving to work I said to my rider, "If I were superstititous I'd go down and meet Connie coming in on the Lurline this morning. I dreamed last night she was on it."

She wasn't, but after a hiatus of seven or eight months there was a letter from her. A letter she had written ten days earlier in Michigan, sent across country by train plus four and half days by boat. So how could my intuition or hunch or ESP or whatever have zeroed in on the day it was to arrive?

Other times my dreams have been prophetic. Often when in the grip of a new romance I would dream of the current heartthrob the night before receiving his letter (mostly they seemed to be distant romeos — geographically, of course). Another time years later when I was living in California brother Bob was visiting at the time of Cassius Clay's first fight for the championship. Having read a good article about him in SPORTS ILLUSTRATED, I was very interested in his career and joined in any discussion of his chances.

The morning of the fight I got up and said to Bob, "Put your money on Clay. He'll win in the fifth." What a lot of jeers and ribbing this brought on, but I stuck to my story.

After all I had dreamed of a sports page with four-inch headlines, CLAY IN THE FIFTH.

At work I wanted to share the good word with everyone but they turned deaf ears. What a pity I didn't know any Las Vegas book makers - or even a Santa Barbara bookie. Best I could get out of Bob was 2 to 1 (he's a real sport!)

The fight came on that night and I watched with a curious mixture of fatalism and nerves - would my hunch prove out or was it a dud? The fifth round came - and went with the challenger still on his feet and Bob began massaging his palms in expectation of my money.

"Don't be in a hurry," I stalled without knowing why.

But it *was* Clay in the fifth! His opponent could not answer the bell for the next round, the sixth, and so the record books all show it was CLAY IN THE FIFTH. For my prescience I won a princely ten dollars.

ESP or whatever it is called certainly makes for easier living. It guides you toward parking spaces, discourages you from doing something that's all wrong right then, in short inkles what you should do when and where, maybe why. The current is not turned on all the time, thereby making it real sporting to pick the genuine flashes from the duds. Come to think of it, that might be the difference between folks like Uncle Jim and the black cat that rode him all his life and others for whom the living is easy. But whatever it is it's a great asset.

XXVI

After Pearl Harbor things got pretty dull there in Hawaii. Martial law had been declared immediately by the Military Governor which really put a damper on everything. Curfew was at 6 p.m. with no unauthorized personnel on the street afterward. Liquor sales were curtailed and rationed (I'm not sure I'd ever bought a bottle of booze before in my life but after that I had to line up with everyone else to get my allotment.)

Things got so dull, in fact, everyone almost welcomed an airraid alarm (for what always turned out to be friendly planes) to liven things up. Fortunately my happiest activities took place in the daytime. Horseback riding out at the stable where I had leased a horse helped me keep my bearings.

Hawaii by then had become not just an armed camp but an arsenal. Army intelligence had learned the Japanese were preparing a mammoth armada, not just a puny little strike force like hit Pearl, but for a major onslaught against the Islands. Most citizens were not aware of this though it only needed a sensitive nature to know there was something brewing.

After December 7th a line had been drawn around Oahu some blocks in from the beach and everyone living between there and the ocean must evacuate in case of an invasion. We were told to get enough basic supplies for two weeks to keep in our cars - food, warm blankets, spare clothing.

Nothing had been said about these evacuation kits for many weeks, maybe months, but newspapers began running notices like Have You Checked Your Evacuation Kit Lately? Would you recognize the evacuation signal? The would-be invaders were approaching, and soon the news broke and the papers were full of it. However, not one breath was there on the radio - one would think Hawaii was floating in a peaceful, sunlit sea with no evildoers within thousands of miles instead of just out there within our radio signal.

Being with the Red Cross was an added advantage as much classified information with its good news and its heartbreaks came through our office. One could have gotten the vapors at thinking the invaders were so close the radio was silent about it, that they were so close our forces were even using land-based aircraft in the Battle of Midway. If the fortunes of war went against us the entire chain of islands (once called the "loveliest fleet of islands anchored in any ocean") would have become one POW camp.

Life went on though: we went to work; we came home; we snatched what recreation we could. Mine continued to be riding although after one month I had given up my leased mount. The stable was out by the polo field near the bridle paths in Kapiolani Park, a large area now well fortified.

One day riding around there I thought smugly, "I'm glad I come from a good American family so I'll not be suspect like so many others in the witchhunt of war hysteria. Famous last thoughts!

The Lyons have always been a family of slickers willing to pull a "fast one" (but never dishonest) if the opportunity offered. A few days later at work a young man with the FBI who had lived at Beach Walk Inn while I was there came into our office, one flight down from his own.

"Miss Lyons?" he queried soberly with a grave face.

Some smart retort was on my lips but I resisted, "Yes."

"Do you know anyone in," he looked at his notes, "Tarzana, California?"

"Yes, my sister and her family and my mother and father live there."

"I have here a statement that you have been communicating with them in code."

"Code! Why I wouldn't," once a smart aleck, always a smart aleck, "I wouldn't know a code if I caught one."

Never a smile, in fact he was possibly a mite sterner. I shaped up in a hurry.

"I don't know what you're talking about."

Again he consulted his notes. "Did you ever hear from your sister that if you were returning to the mainland to cable 'Happy Birthday, Mike' if you were landing in San Francisco and 'Happy Birthday, Pat' for Los Angeles?"

"No, I did not."

Memory caught up with me then. A week earlier I had sent them a cablegram in reply to my sister's asking if I approved selling our dear Island which I had always said was to be mine. Being of frugal nature I realized that there were several words still unused, so as mine had broken I added "Expedite luminous dial Baby Ben," and being still frugal I counted and found there were three unexpended words.

Never, never would I convict a man on circumstantial evidence. My older nephew's birthday was to be that Sunday, so I tacked on a "Happy birthday, Pat."

The FBI had intercepted Patricia's letter with her merry little suggestion and was just waiting for me to make a move, which in my youth and innocence I did.

"A-ha!" they must have thought. "Here is the completion of the dastardly act."

True, I had been thinking about returning to California where good Red Cross help was woefully short. And the boredom of martial law and nothing else to do but work was getting me down while every day that passed, my already aged mother and dad, aged an extra month imagining an enemy bomb parting my blonde hair.

"Well, it was his birthday," I said stoutly. "Here, here's his mother's last letter saying, 'Sunday was Pat's birthday but we didn't do anything — in fact, he made his own birthday cake.' "

Still my erstwhile friend didn't seem convinced.

"You can cable the Ann Arbor, Michigan, city clerk for his birthdate if you want."

"I think you had better come up to headquarters with me now."

"Just a moment. I'll have to tell my superior."

To make sure I didn't slide down a drainpipe or jump out a window he stepped to the door to keep me in sight. I rushed into the office.

"Oh, boss, I've got to go upstairs to the FBI. If I'm not back in two hours call me at Sand Island." (The internment center.)

Trying to look as nonchalant as the proverbial cigarette characters I followed him to the elevator and thence into the Star Chamber. What had happened to my "good

American family?" Where were my Adams forebears now that the chips were down?

My "friend" talked first with the big boss, who then took me on.

"Mr. (how could I have forgotten *that* name) is convinced that you are not guilty of any wrong-doing. You do realize, of course, that the movement of ships in wartime is classified. Therefore, I am sure you would not wish to implicate two good Irish names like Pat and Mike. Henceforth you will refrain from any mention of them by name in any message. Understood?"

Understood! For the next few months before I boarded an Army transport in November, 1942, to zigzag back to the coast I had to limit any reference to my sister's progeny as "the boys," "my nephews," "the kids," "the twerps," anthing but their names.

My arrival was accordingly unheralded but the occasion for much rejoicing. Later when conversation began to lag Nonie said.

"Snooks, why didn't you cable me you were coming like I wrote?"

I let her have both barrels which silenced her briefly.

"Maybe those folks I heard about sent the message verbally and not in a letter," she said thoughtfully. "Yes, that must have been it."

"Well, I never got your letter. Wondered at the time how come you'd missed a week without any explanation."

Years later, sometime after the blessed peace had come, I received in my mail a much stamped, pasted and over-pasted letter with bold printing thereon. "Delayed by Censor." I almost was too.

XXVII

I knew that the years were passing, if nothing else my own mirror told me, but Mother and Dad had always been the Pole Star to all of us. By now the folks had come to live with my sister and her family in Southern California. They were both old, pretty well into their eighties.

And in the fullness of time Dad needed new shoes. When he was a boy a cow had stepped on his instep, so for the last how-many years he could only wear a particular shoe made by the Chippeway Falls Shoe Company of Chippeway Falls, Wisconsin. And bless Bess if a firm in the farthest reaches of Los Angeles didn't carry them.

One day when I was down from Santa Barbara an expedition was mounted to search out the Chippeway Falls outlet in East Los Angeles or somewhere a long, long ways from the San Fernando Valley. We were ushered in and seated.

"My Dad needs new shoes -" my sister began.

"I've always worn your shoes so I wrote the company to find a dealer out here."

It didn't take a very smart salesman to see that what Dad wanted was another pair of black business men's oxfords like he was wearing. Once those restrictions were accepted there was not a great deal of variety and he had only to bring out a couple of pair to insure a good fit.

"Here, sir, if you'll just slip this one on for size," the man murmured as his shoehorn slid Dad's long, narrow foot into the shiny shoe that still smelled of new leather.

Dad just sat there uncertainly until Nonie bent down and felt of the toe. Pressing on the cap and the two bunion points she queried him as to how they felt.

"OK, I guess."

"Why don't you get up and walk around in them a bit?" I suggested and he obediently followed my suggestion.

My heart squeezed down when I realized that our positions were reversed: Dad was the child and my sister and I the adults. The sale was soon completed except for the eager salesman's final pitch.

"We're having a special sale on these now, Mr. Lyons - a second pair for half price if you'd be interested."

I had my mouth open to say "thanks but no thanks." At eighty-seven who needed two pairs of new shoes?

"Yes, I think I would," Dad said matter-of-factly. "How much will they come to?"

Nonie and I looked at each other with barely concealed laughter though our eyes misted with love for this great old man. Buying two pair of shoes at eighty-seven. Now that's optimism!

L'envoi

Writing this book has been a bittersweet labor of love — all of the principals are gone but Bob and me and only Connie and Kit are left in supporting roles. Recreating the past has been sweet, remembering all my dear ones and reliving our times, both happy and sad, together — bitter, for I know it is only a shadow. Many years ago Tennyson said it better: "So sad, so sweet, the days that are no more."